PLATO

On the Trial and Death of Socrates

PLATO

On the Trial and Death of Socrates

Euthyphro, Apology, Crito, Phaedo

Translated into English
With an Introduction and Prefatory Notes
by
LANE COOPER

ὁ δὲ ἀνεξέταστος βίος οὐ βιωτὸς ἀνθρώπῳ.
The unexamined life is not worth living.

—*Apology* 38 a

Cornell Paperbacks

Cornell University Press

Ithaca and London

International Standard Book Number 0-8014-9049-9

PRINTED IN THE UNITED STATES OF AMERICA

To

Preface

This book was meant to accompany after an interval the volume of translations from Plato which the Oxford University Press of New York was good enough to publish for me in the year 1938; my aim was thwarted by an international situation which need not be discussed. Thanks to the loyal generosity of my friend and former pupil, John D. Hertz, Jr., now I am able and happy to have the present volume appear with the imprint of the Cornell University Press; this is a way in which Mr. Hertz, as an alumnus of Cornell University, has wished to pay a tribute of thanks to his Alma Mater. His generous gift has made it possible also to reissue in the series of Cornell Studies in English a work of mine that has long been out of print, called *Methods and Aims in the Study of Literature*.

In this Preface let me say a few things which I wished to say in relation to the four dialogues which are here presented, but could not very well fit into any other part of the book.

One is that we ought not to relish the comparison which is often made off-hand between Socrates and our Lord Jesus Christ. There seem to be interesting parallels between the death of Christ and that of Socrates, and there may be some advantage in noting such parallels, so long as we do not forget the essential difference. A Christian simply must observe that difference, and a neo-pagan will find it if he looks close enough. For example, let us all look at the last words of Socrates and the last words of Christ. Socrates at the end asks Crito to sacrifice a cock for him to Aesculapius the god of healing; no doubt because he, Socrates, is at length to be healed for good. His soul will now be freed from the miserable clog of the body (see below, pp. 106, 192). According to Matthew the last words of Christ were an echo of Psalm 22; and the record of Mark is the same. With John, the last words were 'It is finished'—the work of the Poet of the world on earth. Luke gives evidence of a larger array of sayings from the Cross; with him, the last words are an echo of Psalm 31: 'Father, into thy hands I commend my spirit.' No pagan could say it.

When that difference is granted, then the main point of resemblance between Christ and any other teacher lies in the relation of the group that gathers about the leader, the disciples, to the central figure and to one another. Here, too, in the mutual relations, there are differences to be noted. There was no such bond between the followers of Socrates when he had died as is clearly evinced among the followers of Christ after the Resurrection. There could not be. But there is some value in listing a number of, humanly speaking, the comparable groups. Note, then, first of all the followers of Pythagoras. Thereafter note the circle of Socrates, of Plato, of Epicurus, of Milton, of Port Royal, of Dr. Johnson. Note also before Christ and His disciples their nearest parallel in the disciples of John. And note that after Christ, and in the Christian heritage, the groups, as those of Milton, Johnson, and Port Royal, have in them a spirit which no pagan group could have. Yet one must not forget that, apart from Hebraism, Platonism is the best thing that preceded Christianity, and in a sense prepared the ground for it, and in a hundred ways has been taken up, along with the gains of Aristotle, into the fabric of Christianity in mediaeval and modern times.

A second point concerns the motto on the title-page; perhaps no better motto could be found for that position, but it almost made room there for another maxim, from St. Edmund of Abingdon (d. 1240):

A man should live as if he were going to die to-morrow, but study as if he were going to live for ever.

Let that Socratic and Christian sentiment stand for the motto of this Preface, and an envoy of my little book as it goes forth into the world.

Let it stand also as a recommendation to young readers of this book that they proceed with the study of Greek literature and philosophy in the original tongue; that they go on with Greek if they already have begun it, or begin that study now if as yet they lack a knowledge of Greek. A translator, if any one, should know whether his translation will suffice for a student who wishes to have a solid basis for the study of philosophy. It will not suffice. Translations of Plato effect their highest service when they lead the reader back to Plato himself in his own matchless Greek.

In a scholarly way my principal debt in this book is, first, to the admirable work of French editors and translators in the editions of Plato published by the Association Guillaume Bude. My second great debt is to the work on Plato by the late John Burnet, but in particular to his edition of *Phaedo,* which is several times mentioned throughout the present volume. It gives me pleasure also to thank four of my pupils, Professor Caplan and Professor Hutton, now my colleagues, and Miss Irene Samuel, for their helpful criticism of the translations and introductory matter, and, above all, Professor Pritchard, of Washington and Jefferson College, who read all the translations through in a careful comparison with the Greek text to their great advantage.

LANE COOPER

Ithaca, New York,
   Dec. 14, 1940.

Contents

A List of Dates

Including Dates that Concern Plato

c. 1068 B. C. Codrus reigns; paternal ancestor of Plato.

? 950–900 Floruit of Homer.

? 750 Floruit of Hesiod.

c. 640 Birth of Solon; belonged to Plato's line on the maternal side.

c. 624 Birth of Thales.

? 590 Floruit of Anaximander.
Birth of Xenophanes.

? 580 Floruit of Anaximenes.
Birth of Pythagoras.

c. 570 Floruit of Aesop.

c. 558 Death of Solon.
Birth of Simonides.

c. 546 Death of Thales.

529 Death of Cyrus.

c. 525 Birth of Aeschylus.

c. 524 Birth of Themistocles.

522 (or 518) Birth of Pindar.

521 Darius I begins to reign.

519 Birth of Xerxes I.

c. 510 Birth of Parmenides.

c. 500 Death of Pythagoras.
Floruit of Heraclitus.
Floruit of Phrynicus.
Floruit of Epicharmus.
Birth of Anaxagoras.
Birth of Pericles.

496 Birth of Sophocles.

490 Battle of Marathon.

486 Death of Darius I.

486/5 Xerxes I begins to reign.

c. 485 (? or *c.* 490) Birth of Empedocles.

Birth of Gorgias.
Birth of Protagoras.

c. 480 Birth of Herodotus.
Birth of Euripides.

480 Battle of Thermopylae.
Battle of Salamis.

479 Battle of Plataea.

469 Birth of Socrates.

468 Death of Simonides.

c. 460 Floruit of Zeno of Elea.
Birth of Thucydides.
Birth of Democritus.
Anaxagoras goes to Athens for thirty years.

459 Death of Themistocles.

456 Death of Aeschylus.

? 454 Birth of Aristophanes.

c. 446 Birth of Agathon.

c. 442 (or *c.* 438) Death of Pindar.

440 Floruit of Sophron.

436 Birth of Isocrates.

431 Peloponnesian war begins.

c. 430 Floruit of Prodicus.
Floruit of Hippias of Elis.
Birth of Xenophon.
Surrender of Potidaea.

429 Death of Pericles.

c. 428 Death of Anaxagoras.

428/7 Accepted date of birth of Plato.

427 *Banqueters*, first comedy of Aristophanes.

c. 425 Death of Herodotus.
Death of Empedocles.

423 *Clouds* of Aristophanes takes

third place after Ameipsias'
Connos.
421 Peace of Nicias.
? *c.* 420 Death of Ariston, father of
Plato.
419 Peloponnesian war resumed.
416 Floruit of Agathon.
415–413 Sicilian expedition.
414 *Birds* of Aristophanes.
c. 412 Birth of Diogenes.
c. 408 Birth of Dion, brother-in-law
of Dionysius II.
406 Battle of Arginusae.
Death of Euripides.
Death of Sophocles.
405 Battle of Aegospotami.
Frogs of Aristophanes.
Dionysius of Syracuse established.
404 Peloponnesian war ends with
the downfall of Athens.
404–371 Supremacy of Sparta in
Greece.
c. 400 Death of Agathon.
Death of Thucydides.
399 Death of Socrates.
Plato in Megara.
? 395 Floruit of Xenarchus, son of
Sophron.
Floruit of Alaxemanos of
Teos.
395 Corinthian war begins.
394 Battle of Coronea.
392 *Ecclesiazusae* of Aristophanes.
c. 391—Period of Plato's earlier
travels.
c. 390 Floruit of Eucleides.
c. 388 Plato visits Italy and Sicily.
388 *Plutus* of Aristophanes.
387 Plato returns from Sicily to
Athens.

c. 386 Plato founds the Academy.
386 Corinthian war ends.
384 Birth of Aristotle.
c. 384 Birth of Demosthenes.
377 Second Athenian confederacy.
376 Death of Gorgias.
c. 375 (or later) Death of Aristophanes.
371 Battle of Leuctra.
c. 371 Birth of Theophrastus.
368 Death of Dionysius I.
Dionysius II succeeds to the
tyranny.
Dion asks Plato to visit Sicily.
367 Aristotle enters the Academy.
366 Plato returns from his second
visit to Sicily.
c. 365 Death of Perictione, mother
of Plato.
362 Plato revisits Sicily.
Battle of Mantinea.
362 Plato returns to Athens.
359 Accession of Philip.
357–5 Social war.
357 Dionysius II expelled by
Dion.
c. 355 Death of Xenophon.
354 (or 353) Dion assassinated.
348/7 Accepted date of death of
Plato.
c. 342 Birth of Menander.
338 Death of Isocrates.
323 Death of Diogenes.
322 Death of Demosthenes.
Death of Aristotle.
c. 300 Birth of Herodas.
c. 292 Death of Menander.
287 Death of Theophrastus.
270 Floruit of Theocritus.
250 Death of Herodas.
A. D. 529 Schools of Athens closed by
order of Justinian.

PLATO
On the Trial and Death of Socrates

Introduction

The four dialogues here translated concern the trial and death of Socrates, and hence belong together, though *Euthyphro* is hard to place among them. The other three are ideally conjoined; somehow it is not ideally in close relation to any one of them, nor to all three. It does not seem to have been written with them in mind, and may have been composed as an afterthought, or at a time somewhat remote from the time or times of their composition. If we regarded the dialogues as matter of fact and history, *Euthyphro* would, of course, come first; and placing it first, in accord with an external sequence of events, with chronology more than with imagination, gets it out of the way, provides a lucid enough order for most of the readers who will use this book, and allows the *Apology, Crito,* and *Phaedo* then to produce their cumulative effect, their artistic effect, emotional as well as intellectual, which Plato surely desired to produce in the reader.

Moreover, for a first reading of these four dialogues it would be bad to take up *Euthyphro* just after witnessing the end of Socrates' earthly career. That would be like witnessing the satyr-drama in a tetralogy after the close of a tripartite tragedy; on the stage the quasi-comic treatment of a tragic theme, after the fear and final pity of part three, must not seldom have worked a revulsion in spectators of the more sensitive type. The emotional anticlimax was avoided when the satyr-play came first; and it is gratifying to observe the evidence for a recent view of scholars that, in the performance of Greek tetralogies, this anomalous survival from the primitive drama could on occasion be presented first.

So much for the order of the dialogues in this volume. The matter allows us to mention others. First, the relation, not of *Euthyphro* alone, to tragi-comedy, for many of Plato's Socratic conversations deal in mixed emotions; though, amongst the four we here translate, *Euthyphro* may well have most resemblance to the satyr-drama, a literary species of which, after all, not very much is known. Sometimes the comic element predominated in such dramas, as in Sophocles' *Ichneutae,* sometimes the serious, as in Euripides' *Alcestis.* That Plato at times had the species in mind may be inferred from the remarks of Alcibiades in the *Symposium* on the likeness between Socrates and the Sileni, and from other passages containing hints of a resemblance between him and a good satyr.

Of course we must not push the parallel too hard between a dialogue like *Euthyphro* and the satyr-drama, nor between Platonic dialogues in general and drama whether of a tragic, a comic, or an intermediate serio-comic type. Yet we may mention the grouping, in later antiquity, of Plato's works according to a series of tetralogies. This was done in the reign of Tiberius by Thrasyllus the grammarian. He grouped the Platonic dialogues in nine tetralogies, the first group in fact consisting of *Euthyphro, Apology, Crito,* and *Phaedo,* in that order. The ancient groupings by fours do not satisfy us now, and not merely because they included dialogues which Plato did not write. No grouping of these works is satisfactory if it tends to obscure the independence of each individual work of Plato as a separate artistic whole. And that statement must apply also to the *Apology, Crito,* and *Phaedo,* however naturally they fall together. Each one of them must be regarded as a separate artistic unit. As for other dialogues that we might bring into a loose conjunction with them, with the *Apology* for instance, *Gorgias* [1] would make as good a companion piece as *Euthyphro,* or doubtless, in the minds of some, a better. While *Euthyphro* is linked to the *Apology* through its theme, the nature of religion, and its reference to Socrates' impending trial on a charge of irreligion, the dialogue of *Gorgias* on means and end in speaking is closely linked to the method of Socrates' defence, and throughout that dialogue the reader has, more than in *Euthyphro,* a sense of a danger lying in the path of Socrates, the mortal danger in his way of

[1] See the present writer's volume of translations including *Gorgias* with *Ion, Phaedrus,* and *Symposium* as a fairly natural group of four (noted above in the Preface, p. vi).

living, if ever he were put on trial before the State. There are, however, many relations between still other dialogues of Plato and those that are here presented; the *Apology,* for instance, well illustrates also the principles of eloquence that Socrates lays down and clarifies in *Phaedrus*. In fact, both Plato and his translator would naturally desire the student of any single dialogue to read freely in other works of a similar cast, if only for the light such reading throws upon the nature of the literary, philosophic dialogue.

Here, then, it seems appropriate to append a number of remarks upon this literary type.[2] The dialogue as a type is obviously related to epic poetry and the drama. The Homeric epic poems are a mixture of narration and dialogue in which there seems to be less of the utterance of the poet, and more exchange of speeches by the agents in the poem, than actually is the case. In a rough estimate, our lamented friend the late Samuel E. Bassett said: 'The impersonal narrative, chiefly the account of action, objectively presented, occupies one-fifth of the poems, the speeches three-fifths, and the direct personal utterance of the poet, or his interpretation or explanation which the objective narrative cannot give, one-fifth.'[3] A drama, on the other hand, would seem to be entirely made up of speeches, or at all events a dramatic poet like Sophocles utters nothing in his own person throughout a play. In this respect a dialogue of Plato is like a drama; the author does not appear in it as a speaker. A drama, however, has elements that neither epic poem nor dialogue possesses; when duly exhibited on the stage, it has a direct appeal to our outward senses. We see and hear the actors, and if there are music and dancing, we see and hear them too. The whole drama may be regarded as a continuous spectacle. If it be an opera or a musical comedy, the music too may be regarded as an element or vital tissue that runs

---

[2] The subject is one I have discussed before in several places; see *Two Views of Education* (Yale University Press, 1922); *Evolution and Repentance* (Cornell University Press, 1935); the volume of translations already referred to (Oxford University Press, 1938); and an address entitled *Our Plato,* published in *The Classical Bulletin* 16 (1940), 25-7, 32. It is impossible to treat the subject again without some repetition of thought, and very likely that involves some repetition of phrase, but the present treatment has been written without any consultation of the aforesaid sources. See also the list of books below, pp. 193-4.

[3] *The Poetry of Homer,* Berkeley, California, 1938, p. 85.

throughout the piece. But whether the music is continuous or inter-mittent, it is, like spectacle, an element which is not found in a nar-rative poem or a dialogue. Both epic poetry and the dialogue are likely now and then to refer to music or to describe it, and likely to describe a scene, but doing any of these things is different from directly giving us the spectacle and music of a play.

The upshot is that a dialogue differs from both epic poetry and drama in being more purely one thing, and that is dialogue pure and simple. To the four elements which epic poetry, the drama, and the dialogue have in common we shall return hereafter. Here let us merely note that every one of them must have (1) a plot or vital scheme of the whole, and the persons who carry it on must have (2) their characteristic inner natures and (3) corresponding ways of utterance. A person of a certain bias will argue in a certain way; his natural or acquired choices will lead him to use arguments in favor of them, and to win or to antagonize his fellows; there may even be a bias against bias and in favor of deciding all questions by an appeal to reason. This last is the Socratic type of character, and rare. Whereas others have their choices already made, and the arguments follow, the Socratic character, which is often ironic as well, chooses only after sifting out what is noble and just. Finally, the epic poem, drama, or dialogue will be worked out in (4) the diction. As a painter uses line or color to present his object to us, or the musical com-poser embodies his concept in notes, so Homer, Sophocles, or Plato uses language, either metrical or only cadenced, as his medium of ex-pression. These four elements of plot, character, method of reasoning, and diction are called by Aristotle *muthos, ethos, dianoia,* and *lexis;* they are basic in any work of literary art; and we may add that the Greek terms, when properly understood, are at once more inclusive and precise, and more useful in the technique of interpretation and criticism, than any corresponding terms in English. To a study of these four elements as they are found in the Platonic dialogue we shall return.

Meanwhile let us briefly consider the relation of the dialogue to other literary species in another way.

In time, the dialogue comes relatively late among the species of

Greek art. Of the great outstanding types, of course, the epics of Homer come first. It is customary to speak of these narrative poems, and generally of simple narration in verse or prose, as 'objective,' not inward or deeply spiritual, nor yet mainly for the intellect; in other words, not 'subjective.' Greek drama, which developed later, is obviously more subjective than the epic poem, and Greek tragedy is more deeply spiritual, above all in the lyric parts; while comedy, at all events the comedy of Aristophanes, is in its great formative ideas, and apart from its sheer hilarity, a thing meant rather for the intellect. Both tragedy and comedy are said to be midway between the most subjective types of composition and the least, or to combine subjective with objective elements, leaning now to this side, and again to that. Thus Aeschylean tragedy, in its closer relation to Homer, is more objective than the tragedy of Euripides, which obviously has more problems for the intellect; while Sophocles attains the golden mean between the poles of an objective action and deep emotion, an inward impulse sharply and objectively delineated on the open stage. The most subjective type of poetry is the lyric, now more reflective and again more passionate and emotional in spirit; and it is the choral parts of the drama, the lyrical parts, that lend Greek drama most of its subjectivity; the main bulk of Greek lyric poetry is found in the drama. The lyrics of Greek tragedy are of the heart and the imagination; those of Greek comedy, as it is known to us through Aristophanes, evince the play of wit and fancy.

In time, as tragedy and comedy follow epic poetry, so comedy in its main development comes after tragedy; and the Platonic dialogue, in spirit more allied perhaps to the philosophic comedy of Epicharmus, may yet be described as the next great literary type struck out by the Greek genius after the comedies of Aristophanes. The dialogue, in fact, as a flourishing species, may be regarded as contemporaneous with, and heavily indebted to, the later plays of that great comic author, and related also to the works of his fellows. For one thing, it seems that the comic poets preceded the dialogue in the use of Socrates as main personage in a work of literary art. Witness not only the *Clouds* of Aristophanes, but the *Connos* of Ameipsias as well, two plays exhibited in the same dramatic competition. And again, the *agon* or debate, as for instance the debate between the Unjust Logos and the Just in the *Clouds,* is allied in nature to the dialogue of Plato. More serious dialogues like the *Apology, Crito,* and *Phaedo* obviously are related to Greek tragedy. According to tradition, young Plato tried his hand at writing tragedies before he came into close associa- tion with the master, Socrates, and, now sharing his dislike of the drama, destroyed them.

In its own development, and apart from comedy, the dialogue, or in particular the 'Socratic conversation,' as Aristotle calls it,[4] was not the invention of Plato (428/7–*c*.348 B.C.[5]). It seems that the first writer to compose Socratic conversations was Alexamenos of Teos (*fl.* ?395 B.C.). What relation his dialogues bore to the work of his successors, including Plato, we have no means of knowing. More important surely was the relation of Plato's work to the actual habit of Socrates, throughout his life, of sifting out the truth in conversa- tion by an orderly method of question and answer. There is also an important relation between the dialogue and the prose mime or short artistic, half-dramatic conversation of the comic, sometimes vulgar, sort, at all events in imitation of the life and speech of ordinary men and women, persons, as Wordsworth would say, of humble and rustic estate. The general reader will gain a fairly just impression of the mime from Matthew Arnold's translation of the Fifteenth Idyl of Theocritus.

The dialogue was brought to a state of perfection by Plato. That some of his contemporaries and successors wrote good dialogues may be inferred from the number of such works which were traditionally ascribed to him, and included with all that is genuinely his, but which cannot be by him. The same inference may be drawn from disputes about the authenticity of excellent dialogues, as *Ion,* which may have been written by Plato, or may come from an unknown hand. Aristotle wrote dialogues of which we know by hearsay only or through frag- ments; they are likely to have approached the less dramatic mode of Plato's later works. Of the more dramatic sort, the *Apology* takes the

---

[4] *Poetics* 1.1447 [b] 11; compare Aristotle, Frag. 61 (Rose) from Athenaeus 11.505.
[5] Or he may have been born three years earlier.

leading place, though the close of *Phaedo* is still more tragic. But whether in the more dramatic or the more reflective sort, the dialogues of Plato are the most eminent specimens of their kind throughout the history of Western letters, and have had an influence so deep and wide that, we may say, without Plato the modern dialogue of Galileo, Berkeley, and the rest of an innumerable throng, would never have existed; nor would the dialogue of Lucian, offspring of the shorter ancient dialogue and the mime, nor, of course, such followers of Lucian as Landor.

The main literary species which the Greek genius produced or developed after the dialogue were the New Comedy, which, however, had its roots in Epicharmus, Crates, and the latest plays of Aristophanes; the Idyl, which for us means the poems of Theocritus, Bion, and Moschus; and, if we may call prose poetry poetical, the novel or romance. The New Comedy stands also under the influence of Theophrastus and Aristotle, and hence of Plato. And the Greek romances, partly influenced by the New Comedy, go back for their main influence to the *Odyssey* of Homer. Thus we come full circle in the growth of literary species to the point where we began; and all the others throw some light upon the dialogue, as does it on them. It is because we do regard the cadenced prose of Plato as poetical, and his imaginative structure and dramatic characterization as even more so, that we may, like Aristotle, treat the dialogue among the kinds of poetry, and set forth its relation to them as we have done. The relation of the dialogue to types of Greek prose is a matter of more concern to specialists in the study of Greek than to the author or the reader of any translation.

We return to the constituents of a dialogue. In a work of art, and of literary art in prose or verse, the governing idea of the whole must be the cause and explanation of all other details. For a dialogue we may well give to the march of the whole the name of *logos;* it is this that is running in the mind of the author as he elaborates the parts of his work, down to the last iota. It corresponds to the *muthos* ('myth') or plot which as Aristotle says is the soul of a play. It is like the plan of a building or a garden, like the living skeleton and vital organs of a human being, like the structure which involves the meaning of a sonnet, like the design of a painting. It is like the plot or *muthos* of an epic poem.

The *logos* comes first in importance, but may not come first in time. As in tragedy the traditional persons may stand out beforehand, and the special action of a given play may then grow out of their wilful tragic choices, so the writer of a dialogue may begin with a man called Socrates and another man called Euthyphro, and then a situation and an argument can be developed. But the march of the argument determines the nature of that special dialogue, and makes it differ from the rest of our Socratic conversations; or if any one insists that the relation between the two speakers gives rise to the whole work of art, we may then reply that the interrelation between the speakers, or between any other two or more parts of the whole, belongs to the plot or *logos*, and not to character or *ethos*, or to *dianoia* or to *lexis*.

Ethos will come next in order of importance, so far as we can separate it from *dianoia*—at least in the more dramatic sort of dialogue. The habit of the speakers, their tendency to choose a certain line of thought, come, we say, next in order of importance after the *logos* of the whole as conceived by the mind of the author. Socrates' determination to defend himself in one way rather than another gives rise to the speeches of which the *Apology* is made up; so Plato works it out.

The irony of Socrates in actual life was accepted by Plato for the literary dialogue, and by other writers as well; so other traits of the historical Socrates were accepted by the authors of imaginary conversations; the admixture of reality always makes a work of art more credible and persuasive.

Dianoia comes next. It may be thought that in the less dramatic sort of dialogue *dianoia* must take precedence over *ethos*. And, off-hand, the dialogue as a literary type seems all made up of speech and argument. But so also does a drama. His *logos* and his characters determined, the author of a dialogue has for his business the writing of a set of speeches; so far his task in no way differs from the task of a playwright. Accordingly, at this point all we need to add is that *dianoia* is a necessary element of a dialogue, as are the *logos* and the *ethos;* they are, like the *lexis,* inevitable constituents of this kind of writing; but a well-conceived *logos* will give rise to suitable speeches in a correct succession, while clever individual speeches will not make a dialogue.

The *logos* runs throughout the dialogue, and penetrates every detail. *Ethos* similarly is continuous throughout, pervasive. So obviously is the *dianoia.* That the same is true of *lexis* goes without saying, for the whole is clothed in language. Language is the medium in which the *logos, ethos,* and *dianoia* are embodied. In a Platonic dialogue the four are bound together in such wise that damage is done to each and all when we try to think of them apart; and yet there is advantage in analysis when the effort needful to the making of it meets its end in a clear and final synthesis of the many in the one—when we see the whole in the parts and the parts in the whole.

Little need here be said of *lexis* in detail. Masterly in construction, in presenting character, in conducting argument, Plato was a master of syntax, phrase, and cadence. His mastery of cadence is attested by the ancient critics. If his opulence, or on occasion violence, of figures of thought and speech drew upon him an occasional censure from a critic such as 'Longinus,' still the richness and beauty of his metaphor and cadence, and withal the clarity and simplicity of his medium, the diction as a whole, have excited the praise of generations from his own day until now. The main burden of 'Longinus' swells the chorus. Apart from our Sacred Scriptures, Plato is, for substance and expression, the greatest writer of all time.

With regard to *ethos,* he exhibits the one man Socrates in a myriad of lights and contrasts, and therewith a multitude of other men. He has given us also in the *Symposium* that immortal lady Diotima, so strangely like the Wisdom of the Book of Proverbs, and forerunner of the Beatrice of Dante with her modern retinue of earthly women celestial. His good manners extend to his treatment of Socrates' wife Xanthippe; the conception of her as a shrew does not proceed from the writings of Plato. He can give us the *ethos* of a man with a few deft touches; note the skill with which he has presented Socrates' gentle-hearted keeper in prison. Be it noted that the dialogues of

Plato, as should be expected of an Academic leader, are a model of good manners. The character of Socrates is that of an *eirōn*, a type imperfectly suggested by our word 'ironic'; the habitual understatement of an *eirōn* is close to the nature of truth and considerate manners.

As for *dianoia*, it is not to be studied in an Introduction, but by a logical analysis of each dialogue and the scrutiny of Rhetoric; to this end the *Rhetoric* of Aristotle may be specially recommended as a companion to the study of Plato. We may note, however, the free use of paradox and sophistry in the march toward final truth in any dialogue, and some quibbling and 'eristic' along the way for fun. Plato was a master of that sort of thing, knew what he did, and why, when using it, and was not mastered by it. With him good sense and reason in the end prevail. It must be remembered, though, that Plato aims, not at historical precision and fidelity, but at a truth transcending particular detail, truth universal and poetic, operating in the heart and mind for the ends of life.

We have chosen to call the plot of a dialogue the *logos*, equivalent to the Latin *ratio*, and hence to Middle English *resoun*, the word which Chaucer uses to describe the plan of an artistic whole. If we use the word *logos* for the plot or action of a dialogue conceived of as an organic whole, we may doubtless employ the word *muthos* or 'myth' for a part of the *logos* which constantly appears in a Platonic dialogue, and in general has a very great importance there. Sometimes the element in question is an allegory like the allegory of the Cave in the *Republic*. The word more properly describes the myth of Er in the *Republic*, and the tales which have a similar function in other works of Plato. *Muthos*, however, conveniently represents not only tales of great or lesser import in the dialogues, but, as aforesaid, the allegory of the Cave, and Socrates' account of the flight of the soul in *Phaedrus*.

Plato does, indeed, in *Phaedo* (61 b) make Socrates distinguish between *logoi*, tales that are true, and *muthoi*, tales or accounts for which he cannot certainly vouch; these would be representations of things or events in the future or very remote in heaven above or in the earth beneath, or in the dim and distant past; the stories may be matters of hearsay. For our present end, however, we are warranted in cleaving to our helpful distinction between *logos* for the march or plot of the dialogue as a whole, and *muthos* for this special element in the plot, which, like an *exemplum* in a sermon or any other public speech, may sum up the whole or render the whole, or a part of it, more concrete, vivid, and telling.

The *muthos* of a dialogue, then, is a kind of vital nucleus in which the life of the whole is centred; it is poetical, concrete, of the imagination; when reasoned argument has gone as far as reason can go, the *muthos* supplements the work of reason, and, rising out of it, transcends it, and lifts us out of time and place to the world of eternal truth and beauty.

In general, this element, whether of a lowlier sort or lofty, illuminating a small part or a larger of the whole, lends the interest of story and picture to what otherwise would be dialogue pure and simple. In *Euthyphro* the story has the humble purpose of setting the tune for the dialogue; it is simply the tale of the unlucky slave who perished through the inadvertence of Euthyphro's father, whom the son, accordingly, is moving to indict upon religious grounds; and hence the question of Socrates, What is religion or piety? In the *Apology* we have the tale of Chaerephon's visit to the oracle; he learns that 'no one is wiser than Socrates'; whereupon Socrates undertakes his quest of a man wiser than himself; with the upshot that all other men are seen to be less wise in that they do not know of their own ignorance, whereas he not only does not have what they call wisdom, but knows that he does not. In *Crito* the place of the myth is taken by the apparition of the Laws and their discourse with Socrates. *Phaedo,* of course, has the most elaborate myth of the dialogues presented in this volume, the account of the underworld, the surface on which we live, and the true surface or outer envelope of the whole.

A myth lends a heightened and telling effect to the whole dialogue; but we must remember that the effect of the whole is more important than the significance of any part; that the part is, in itself, always less important than the whole; and that the effect of the whole, if the whole is a true work of art, is always more than the mere sum of all the parts.

What is the effect of a Platonic dialogue? That differs necessarily with every dialogue; the tone or atmosphere of *Euthyphro*, for instance, is different from that of the *Apology* or *Crito*. In general, we may say that the effect of any dialogue upon a cultivated reader, upon a man of good sense, must be what Plato intended. And we have some evidence throughout the ages of the effect which Plato has had upon the wisest and most gifted minds—orators, philosophers, and poets, indeed upon artists of every sort. He has touched and kindled their minds. The effect of reading Plato is exhilaration. Obviously the play of argument in dialogue quickens our mental pace. The dialogues of Plato fill the mind, and set it working. They may be used deliberately to that end by persons who find themselves called upon to produce essays, speeches, introductions, and who do not find the phrases and ideas flowing without some stimulus. As a stimulus Plato is better than wine.

So far as the emotions and the intellect may be considered apart, the effect of his dialogues may be regarded in a dual aspect. The argument is obviously directed at the mental faculties; it asks for thought and stirs the mind. On the side of the emotions, some dialogues (as we have seen) share in the nature of comedy; indeed, the earlier dialogues, which are dramatic, not seldom aim to stir a smile or an academic laugh. Even the more tragic dialogues are not without a comic element; the reference in the *Apology* to Socrates as he is represented in the *Clouds* of Aristophanes provokes a smile, and was meant to do that, in spite of the serious argument which the reference supports. Plato was no Bossuet with his bitter animus towards Moliere. Of course it is clear that the *Apology, Crito,* and *Phaedo* are very like a tragic trilogy. It is also true that all great art is moving, and can move us to tears when it is not concerned with tragic suffering, mortal suspense, or death. Wordsworth has the notion in mind when he tells how a simple flower may give him thoughts that 'lie too deep for tears'; he doubtless felt the tearful emotion even in his denial, and we too feel it. *Sunt lacrimae rerum.* Art thus moves us when it soars above all earthly matters into the eternal realm whither Plato so often transports us.

But in all four dialogues, yet especially in *Phaedo,* we note a distinct intent on Plato's part to work strangely upon mixed emotions by suggesting both laughter and tears. He makes young Phaedo refer to the strangeness of the combination. The mixture was known to Macaulay:

> With weeping and with laughter
>   Still is the story told,
> How well Horatius kept the bridge
>   In the brave days of old.[6]

Nor was the like unknown to Homer; witness the sad parting of Andromache from Hector, and her tearful smiling (*Iliad* 6.484, δακρυόεν γελάσασα), doubtless a favorite passage with Plato as with Macaulay.

And even more the artistic effort of Plato to work on two or more emotions in the reader, and to combine them, will remind us of the like effort of the poet Wordsworth, who says:[7]

A great poet ought, . . . to a certain degree, to rectify men's feelings, to give them new compositions of feeling, to render their feelings more sane, pure, and permanent, in short, more consonant to nature, that is, to eternal nature, and the great moving spirit of things.

Wordsworth's thought here is Platonic. As my friend Charles G. Osgood rightly argues in *The Voice of England*, there is more of Plato in Wordsworth than is commonly supposed; far more, we may add, than is dreamt of by those who know but a few things like the *Ode, Intimations of Immortality*. We may therefore close this Introduction with another testimony from the same poet; it is recorded by Wordsworth's nephew:[8]

I have heard him pronounce that the tragedy of *Othello*, Plato's records of the last scenes of the career of Socrates, and Isaac Walton's *Life of George Herbert*, were in his opinion the most pathetic of human compositions.

---

[6] *Horatius*, last four lines.
[7] Letter to John Wilson, 1800.
[8] *Memoirs of Wordsworth*, by Christopher Wordsworth, 2.482 (London, 1851).

Euthyphro

Euthyphro

Euthyphro is a clear and plain dialogue, rising to no great height of eloquence such as Plato reaches in *Phaedo* or the *Apology*. It needs no long preface or explanation. It is a short dialogue of some 6,000 words in Greek. *Crito*, somewhat shorter, runs to about 4,100 words. In its brevity *Euthyphro* also resembles *Ion* (of about 4,000 words or fewer); and it is like *Ion* too in its use of a telling rhetorical or dialectic device, the insistent repetition of a single question. In *Ion* we meet the repeated question, What does the rhapsode know? What *is* the special province of learning which he controls? The problem is not solved, for according to the trend of the argument Ion can give no satisfying answer. The same device is used by Plato in *Gorgias*. As if the successive answers of each successive speaker had not been uttered, Socrates returns again and again to ask, What is the special province of Rhetoric, and what special body of knowledge does the rhetorician possess?

In *Euthyphro* the inquiry concerns religion. What *is* religion? What *is* piety? The question is repeatedly put, and Euthyphro gives no real answer. What they are not is made to appear; and the impious nature of Euthyphro in the suit he brings against his father is evident enough. He is an impious pharisee. The religious nature of Socrates is also plainly revealed. That doubtless was a matter of importance to the author of the dialogue. More important still is the result of the discussion as an effect in the mind of the reader, who is led to think insistently on the question of piety, and to consider the difference between the essence of religion and the outward show.

Euthyphro conforms to the type of dialogue in which Socrates pursues his quest after a man who has real knowledge, and who does not rest content with vulgar opinion. The quest is described in the *Apology*. It is a theme that could give rise to many dialogues. *Ion* is another example. And there must have been numerous authors besides Plato who wrote imaginary conversations between Socrates and different kinds of individual possessed of a seeming knowledge, but living only in the atmosphere of commonplace views.

We note also in this dialogue the recognition by Socrates of the established deities that were accredited by Athens. As in the *Apology*, so here, he swears by the gods of the City.

To a Christian, *Euthyphro* can hardly fail to be a little disappointing; but we need not expect from it such concepts of religion as are everywhere found in the Bible; thus (James 1.27): 'Pure religion and undefiled before God and the Father is this: To visit the fatherless and widows in their affliction, and to keep himself unspotted from the world.' And yet Plato in his pagan way has shown his Socrates to be a man who was in the world, but not of it.

Euthyphro

EUTHYPHRO. This, Socrates, is something new? What has taken 2
you from your haunts in the Lyceum, and makes you spend your
time at the Royal porch? You surely cannot have a case at law,
as I have, before the Archon-King.

SOCRATES. My business, Euthyphro, is not what is known at Athens
as a case at law; it is a criminal prosecution.

EUTHYPHRO. How is that? You mean that somebody is prosecuting
you? I never would believe that you were prosecuting anybody
else.

SOCRATES. No indeed.

EUTHYPHRO. Then somebody is prosecuting you?

SOCRATES. Most certainly.

EUTHYPHRO. Who is it?

SOCRATES. I am not too clear about the man myself, Euthyphro. He
appears to me to be a young man, and unknown. I think, however,
that they call him Meletus; and his deme is Pitthos, if you happen
to know any one named Meletus of that deme, a hook-nosed man
with long straight hair, and not much beard.

EUTHYPHRO. I don't recall him, Socrates. But tell me, of what does
he accuse you?

SOCRATES. His accusation? It is no mean charge. For a man of his
age it is no small thing to have settled a question of so much importance. He says, in fact, that he knows the method by which
young people are corrupted, and knows who the persons are that
do it. He is, quite possibly, a wise man, and, observing that my
ignorance has led me to corrupt his generation, comes like a child
to his mother to accuse me to the City. And to me he appears to
be the only one who begins his political activity aright; for the

right way to begin is to pay attention to the young, and make them just as good as possible; precisely as the able farmer will give his attention to the young plants first, and afterwards care for the rest. And so Meletus no doubt begins by clearing us away, the ones who ruin, as he says, the tender shoots of the young; that done, he obviously will care for the older generation, and will thus become the cause, in the highest and widest measure, of benefit to the State. With such a notable beginning, his chances of success look good.

EUTHYPHRO. I hope so, Socrates; but I'm very much afraid it will go the other way. When he starts to injure you, it simply looks to me like beginning at the hearth to hurt the State. But tell me what he says you do to corrupt the young.

SOCRATES. It sounds very queer, my friend, when first you hear it. He says I am a maker of gods; he charges me with making new gods, and not believing in the old ones. These are his grounds for prosecuting me, he says.

EUTHYPHRO. I see it, Socrates. It is because you say that ever and anon you have the spiritual sign! So he charges you in this indictment with introducing novelties in religion, and that is the reason why he comes to court with this slanderous complaint, well knowing how easily such matters can be misrepresented to the crowd. For my own part, when I speak in the assembly about matters of religion, and tell them in advance what will occur, they laugh at me as if I were a madman; and yet I never have made a prediction that did not come true. But the truth is, they are jealous of all such people as ourselves. No, we must not worry over them, but go to meet them.

SOCRATES. Dear Euthyphro, if we were only laughed at, it would be no serious matter. The Athenians, as it seems to me, are not very much disturbed if they think that So-and-so is clever, so long as he does not impart his knowledge to anybody else. But the moment they suspect that he is giving his ability to others, they get angry, whether out of jealousy, as you say, or, it may be, for some other reason.

EUTHYPHRO. With regard to that, I am not very eager to test their attitude to me.

SOCRATES. Quite possibly you strike them as a man who is chary of himself, and is unwilling to impart his wisdom; as for me, I fear I am so kindly they will think that I pour out all I have to every one; and not merely without pay—nay, rather, glad to offer something if it would induce some one to hear me. Well then, as I said just now, if they were going to laugh at me, as you say they do at you, it would n't be at all unpleasant to spend the time laughing and joking in court. But if they take the matter seriously, then there is no knowing how it will turn out. Only you prophets can tell!

EUTHYPHRO. Well, Socrates, perhaps no harm will come of it at all, but you will carry your case as you desire, and I think that I shall carry mine.

SOCRATES. Your case, Euthyphro? What is it? Are you prosecuting, or defending?

EUTHYPHRO. Prosecuting.

SOCRATES. Whom?

EUTHYPHRO. One whom I am thought a maniac to be attacking.   4

SOCRATES. How so? Is it some one who has wings to fly away with?

EUTHYPHRO. He is far from being able to do that; he happens to be old, a very old man.

SOCRATES. Who is it, then?

EUTHYPHRO. It is my father.

SOCRATES. Your father, my good friend?

EUTHYPHRO. Just so.

SOCRATES. What is the complaint? Of what do you accuse him?

EUTHYPHRO. Of murder, Socrates.

SOCRATES. Good heavens, Euthyphro! Surely the crowd is ignorant of the way things ought to go. I fancy it is not correct for any ordinary person to do that [to prosecute his father on this charge], but only for a man already far advanced in point of wisdom.

EUTHYPHRO. Yes, Socrates, by Heaven! far advanced!

SOCRATES. And the man your father killed, was he a relative of yours? Of course he was? You never would prosecute your father, would you, for the death of anybody who was not related to you?

EUTHYPHRO.   You amuse me, Socrates. You think it makes a difference whether the victim was a member of the family, or not related, when the only thing to watch is whether it was right or not for the man who did the deed to kill him. If he was justified, then let him go; if not, you have to prosecute him, no matter if the man who killed him shares your hearth, and sits at table with you. The pollution is the same if, knowingly, you associate with such a man, and do not cleanse yourself, and him as well, by bringing him to justice. The victim in this case was a laborer of mine, and when we were cultivating land in Naxos, we employed him on our farm. One day he had been drinking, and became enraged at one of our domestics, and cut his throat; whereupon my father bound him hand and foot, and threw him into a ditch. Then he sent a man to Athens to find out from the seer what ought to be done; meanwhile paying no attention to the man who had been bound, neglecting him because he was a murderer and it would be no great matter even if he died. And that was just what happened. Hunger, cold, and the shackles, finished him before the messenger got back from visiting the seer. That is why my father and my other kin are bitter at me when I prosecute my father as a murderer. They say he did not kill the man, and had he actually done it, the victim was himself a murderer, and for such a man one need have no consideration. They say that for a son to prosecute his father as a murderer is unholy. How ill they know divinity in its relation, Socrates, to what is holy or unholy!

SOCRATES.   But you, by Heaven! Euthyphro, you think that you have such an accurate knowledge of things divine, and what is holy and unholy, that, in circumstances such as you describe, you can accuse your father? You are not afraid that you yourself are doing an unholy deed?

EUTHYPHRO.   Why, Socrates, if I did not have an accurate knowledge
5   of all that, I should be good for nothing, and Euthyphro would be no different from the general run of men.

SOCRATES.   Well then, admirable Euthyphro, the best thing I can do is to become your pupil, and challenge Meletus before the trial comes on. Let me tell him that in the past I have considered it of great importance to know about things divine; and that now, when he asserts that I erroneously put forward my own notions and inventions on this head, I have become your pupil. I could say: 'Come, Meletus, if you agree that Euthyphro has wisdom in such matters, you must admit as well that I hold the true belief, and must not prosecute. If you do not, you must lodge your complaint, not against me, but against my aforesaid master; accuse him of corrupting the elder generation, me and his own father; me by his instruction, his father by correcting and chastising him.' And if he would not yield, would neither quit the suit nor yet indict you rather than myself, then I would say the same in court as when I challenged him!

EUTHYPHRO. Yes, Socrates, by Heaven! if he undertook to bring me into court, I guess I would find out his rotten spot, and our talk there would concern him sooner by a long shot than ever it would me!

SOCRATES. Yes, my dear friend, that I know, and so I wish to be your pupil. This Meletus, I perceive, along presumably with everybody else, appears to overlook you, but sees into me so easily and keenly that he has attacked me for impiety. So, in the name of Heaven, tell me now about the matter you just felt sure you knew quite thoroughly. State what you take piety and impiety to be with reference to murder and all other cases. Is not the holy always one and the same thing in every action, and, again, is not the unholy always opposite to the holy, and like itself? And as unholiness does it not always have its one essential form, which will be found in everything that is unholy?

EUTHYPHRO. Yes, surely, Socrates.

SOCRATES. Then tell me. How do you define the holy and the unholy?

EUTHYPHRO. Well then, I say that the holy is what I am now doing, prosecuting the wrongdoer who commits a murder or a sacrilegious robbery, or sins in any other point like that, whether it be your father, or your mother, or whoever it may be. And not to prosecute would be unholy. And, Socrates, observe what a decisive proof

I will give you that such is the law. It is one I have already given to others; I tell them that the right procedure must be not to tolerate the impious man, no matter who. Do not mankind believe that Zeus is the most excellent and just among the gods? And these same men admit that Zeus shackled his own father [Cronus] for swallowing his [other] sons unjustly; and that Cronus in turn had gelded his father [Uranus] for like reasons. But now they are enraged at me when I proceed against my father for wrong-doing; and so they contradict themselves in what they say about the gods and what they say of me.

SOCRATES. There, Euthyphro, you have the reason why the charge is brought against me. It is because, whenever people tell such stories about the gods, I am prone to take it ill; and, so it seems, that is why they will maintain that I am sinful. Well, now, if you who are so well versed in matters of the sort entertain the same beliefs, then necessarily, it would seem, I must give in; for what could we urge who admit that, for our own part, we are quite ignorant about these matters? But, in the name of friendship, tell me! Do you actually believe that these things happened so?

EUTHYPHRO. Yes, Socrates, and things even more amazing, of which the multitude do not know.

SOCRATES. And you actually believe that war occurred among the gods, and there were dreadful hatreds, battles, and all sorts of fearful things like that? Such things as the poets tell of, and good artists represent in sacred places; yes, and at the great Panathenaic festival the robe that is carried up to the Acropolis is all inwrought with such embellishments? What is our position, Euthyphro? Do we say that these things are true?

EUTHYPHRO. Not these things only, Socrates, but, as I just now said, I will, if you wish, relate to you many other stories about the gods, which I am certain will astonish you when you hear them.

SOCRATES. I shouldn't wonder. You shall tell me all about them when we have the leisure at some other time. At present try to tell me more clearly what I asked you a little while ago; for, my friend, you were not explicit enough before when I put the question,

What is holiness? You merely said that what you are now doing is a holy deed—namely, prosecuting your father on a charge of murder.

EUTHYPHRO.   And, Socrates, I told the truth.

SOCRATES.   Possibly. But, Euthyphro, there are many other things that you will say are holy.

EUTHYPHRO.   Because they are.

SOCRATES.   Well, bear in mind that what I asked of you was not to tell me one or two out of all the numerous actions that are holy; I wanted you to tell me what is the essential form of holiness which makes all holy actions holy. I believe you held that there is one ideal form by which unholy things are all unholy, and by which all holy things are holy. Do you remember that?

EUTHYPHRO.   I do.

SOCRATES.   Well then, show me what, precisely, this ideal is, so that, with my eye on it, and using it as a standard, I can say that any action done by you or anybody else is holy if it resembles this ideal, or, if it does not, can deny that it is holy.

EUTHYPHRO.   Well, Socrates, if that is what you want, I certainly can tell you.

SOCRATES.   It is precisely what I want.

EUTHYPHRO.   Well then, what is pleasing to the gods is holy, and what is not pleasing to them is unholy.

7

SOCRATES.   Perfect, Euthyphro! Now you give me just the answer that I asked for. Meanwhile, whether it is right I do not know; but obviously you will go on to prove your statement true.

EUTHYPHRO.   Indeed I will.

SOCRATES.   Come now, let us scrutinize what we are saying. What is pleasing to the gods, and the man that pleases them, are holy; what is hateful to the gods, and the man they hate, unholy. But the holy and unholy are not the same; the holy is directly opposite to the unholy. Isn't it so?

EUTHYPHRO.   It is.

SOCRATES.   And the matter clearly was well stated.

EUTHYPHRO.   I accept it, Socrates; that was stated.

SOCRATES. Was it not also stated, Euthyphro, that the gods revolt and differ with each other, and that hatreds come between them?

EUTHYPHRO. That was stated.

SOCRATES. Hatred and wrath, my friend—what kind of disagreement will produce them? Look at the matter thus. If you and I were to differ about numbers, on the question which of two was the greater, would a disagreement about that make us angry at each other, and make enemies of us? Should we not settle things by calculation, and so come to an agreement quickly on any point like that?

EUTHYPHRO. Yes, certainly.

SOCRATES. And similarly if we differed on a question of greater length or less, we would take a measurement, and quickly put an end to the dispute?

EUTHYPHRO. Just that.

SOCRATES. And so, I fancy, we should have recourse to scales, and settle any question about a heavier or lighter weight?

EUTHYPHRO. Of course.

SOCRATES. What sort of thing, then, is it about which we differ, till, unable to arrive at a decision, we might get angry and be enemies to one another? Perhaps you have no answer ready; but listen to me. See if it is not the following: right and wrong, the noble and the base, and good and bad. Are not these the things about which we differ, till, unable to arrive at a decision, we grow hostile (when we do grow hostile) to each other, you and I and everybody else?

EUTHYPHRO. Yes, Socrates, that is where we differ; on these subjects.

SOCRATES. What about the gods, then, Euthyphro? If, indeed, they have dissensions, must it not be on these subjects?

EUTHYPHRO. Quite necessarily.

SOCRATES. Accordingly, my noble Euthyphro, by your account some gods take one thing to be right, and others take another, and similarly with the honorable and the base, and good and bad. They would hardly be at variance with each other, if they did not differ on these questions. Would they?

EUTHYPHRO. You are right.

SOCRATES. And what each one of them thinks noble, good, and just, is what he loves, and the opposite is what he hates?

EUTHYPHRO. Yes, certainly.

SOCRATES. But it is the same things, so you say, that some of them think right, and others wrong; and through disputing about these 8 they are at variance, and make war on one another. Isn't it so?

EUTHYPHRO. It is.

SOCRATES. Accordingly, so it would seem, the same things will be hated by the gods and loved by them; the same things would alike displease and please them.

EUTHYPHRO. It would seem so.

SOCRATES. And so, according to this argument, the same things, Euthyphro, will be holy and unholy.

EUTHYPHRO. That may be.

SOCRATES. In that case, admirable friend, you have not answered what I asked you. I did not ask you to tell me what at once is holy and unholy; but it seems that what is pleasing to the gods is also hateful to them. Thus, Euthyphro, it would not be strange at all if what you now are doing in punishing your father were pleasing to Zeus, but hateful to Cronus and Uranus, and welcome to Hephaestus, but odious to Hera, and if any other of the gods disagree about the matter, satisfactory to some of them, and odious to others.

EUTHYPHRO. But, Socrates, my notion is that, on this point, there is no difference of opinion among the gods; not one of them but thinks that if a person kills another wrongfully, he ought to pay for it.

SOCRATES. And what of men? Have you never heard a man contending that some one who has killed a person wrongfully, or done some other unjust deed, ought not to pay the penalty?

EUTHYPHRO. Why! there is never any end to their disputes about these matters; it goes on everywhere, above all in the courts. People do all kinds of wrong, and then there is nothing they will not do or say in order to escape the penalty.

SOCRATES. Do they admit wrongdoing, Euthyphro, and, while admitting it, deny that they ought to pay the penalty?

EUTHYPHRO. No, not that, by any means.

SOCRATES. Then they will not do and say quite everything. Unless I am mistaken, they dare not say or argue that if they do wrong they should not pay the penalty. No, I think that they deny wrong-doing. How about it?

EUTHYPHRO. It is true.

SOCRATES. Therefore they do not dispute that anybody who does wrong should pay the penalty. No, the thing that they dispute about is likely to be who is the wrongdoer, what he did, and when.

EUTHYPHRO. That is true.

SOCRATES. Well then, is n't that precisely what goes on among the gods, if they really do have quarrels about right and wrong, as you say they do? One set will hold that some others do wrong, and the other set deny it? For that other thing, my friend, I take it no one, whether god or man, will dare to say—that the wrongdoer should not pay the penalty!

EUTHYPHRO. Yes, Socrates, what you say is true—in the main.

SOCRATES. It is the individual act, I fancy, Euthyphro, that the disputants dispute about, both men and gods, if gods ever do dispute. They differ on a certain act; some hold that it was rightly done, the others that it was wrong. Is n't it so?

EUTHYPHRO. Yes, certainly.

9 SOCRATES. Then come, dear Euthyphro, teach me as well, and let me grow more wise. What proof have you that all the gods think that your servant died unjustly, your hireling who, when he had killed a man, was shackled by the master of the victim, and perished, dying because of his shackles before the man who shackled him could learn from the seers what ought to be done with him? What proof have you that for a man like him it is right for a son to prosecute his father, and indict him on a charge of murder? Come on. Try to make it clear to me beyond all doubt that under these conditions the gods must all consider this action to be right. If you can adequately prove it to me, I will never cease from praising you for your wisdom.

EUTHYPHRO. But, Socrates, that, very likely, would be no small task, although I could indeed make it very clear to you.

SOCRATES. I understand. You think that I am duller than the judges;

obviously you will demonstrate to them that what your father did was wrong, and that the gods all hate such deeds.

EUTHYPHRO. I shall prove it absolutely, Socrates, if they will listen to me.

SOCRATES. They are sure to listen if they think that you speak well. But while you were talking, a notion came into my head, and I asked myself: Suppose that Euthyphro proved to me quite clearly that all the gods consider such a death unjust; would I have come one whit the nearer for him to knowing what the holy is, and what is the unholy? The act in question, seemingly, might be displeasing to the gods; but then we have just seen that you cannot define the holy and unholy in that way; for we have seen that a given thing may be displeasing, and also pleasing, to gods? So on this point, Euthyphro, I will let you off; if you like, the gods shall all consider the act unjust, and they all shall hate it. But suppose that we now correct our definition, and say that what the gods all hate is unholy, and what they love is holy, whereas what some of them love, and others hate, is either both or neither; are you willing that we now define the holy and unholy in this way?

EUTHYPHRO. What is there to prevent us, Socrates?

SOCRATES. Nothing to prevent me, Euthyphro. As for you, see whether when you take this definition you can quite readily instruct me, as you promised.

EUTHYPHRO. Yes, I would indeed affirm that holiness is what the gods all love, and its opposite is what the gods all hate, unholiness.

SOCRATES. Are we to examine this position also, Euthyphro, to see if it is sound? Or shall we let it through, and thus accept our own and others' statement, and agree to an assertion simply when somebody says that a thing is so? Must we not look into what the speaker says?

EUTHYPHRO. We must. And yet, for my part, I regard the present statement as correct.

SOCRATES. We shall soon know better about that, my friend. Now 10 think of this. Is what is holy holy because the gods approve it, or do they approve it because it is holy?

EUTHYPHRO. I do not get your meaning.

SOCRATES. Well, I will try to make it clearer. We speak of what is carried and the carrier, do we not, of led and leader, of the seen and that which sees? And you understand that in all such cases the things are different, and how they differ?

EUTHYPHRO. Yes, I think I understand.

SOCRATES. In the same way what is loved is one thing, and what loves is another?

EUTHYPHRO. Of course.

SOCRATES. Tell me now, is what is carried 'carried' because something carries it, or is it for some other reason?

EUTHYPHRO. No, but for that reason.

SOCRATES. And what is led, because something leads it? And what is seen, because something sees it?

EUTHYPHRO. Yes, certainly.

SOCRATES. Then it is not because a thing is seen that something sees it; but just the opposite: because something sees it, therefore it is seen. Nor because it is led, that something leads it; but because something leads it, therefore it is led. Nor because it is carried, that something carries it; but because something carries it, therefore it is carried. Do you see what I wish to say, Euthyphro? It is this: whenever an effect occurs, or something is effected, it is not the thing effected that gives rise to the effect; no, there is a cause, and then comes this effect. Nor is it because a thing is acted on that there is this effect; no, there is a cause for what it undergoes, and then comes this effect. Don't you agree?

EUTHYPHRO. I do.

SOCRATES. Well then, when a thing is loved, is it not in process of becoming something, or of undergoing something, by some other thing?

EUTHYPHRO. Yes, certainly.

SOCRATES. Then the same is true here as in the previous cases. It is not because a thing is loved that they who love it love it, but it is loved because they love it.

EUTHYPHRO. Necessarily.

SOCRATES. Then what are we to say about the holy, Euthyphro? According to your argument, is it not loved by all the gods?

EUTHYPHRO. Yes.

SOCRATES. Because it is holy, or for some other reason?

EUTHYPHRO. No, it is for that reason.

SOCRATES. And so it is because it is holy that it is loved; it is not holy because it is loved.

EUTHYPHRO. So it seems.

SOCRATES. On the other hand, it is beloved and pleasing to the gods just because they love it?

EUTHYPHRO. No doubt of that.

SOCRATES. So what is pleasing to the gods is not the same as what is holy, Euthyphro; nor, according to your statement, is the holy the same as what is pleasing to the gods; they are two different things.

EUTHYPHRO. How may that be, Socrates?

SOCRATES. Because we are agreed that the holy is loved because it is holy, and is not holy because it is loved. Isn't it so?

EUTHYPHRO. Yes.

SOCRATES. Whereas what is pleasing to the gods is pleasing to them just because they love it, such being its nature and its cause. Its being loved of the gods is not the reason of its being loved.

EUTHYPHRO. You are right.

SOCRATES. But suppose, dear Euthyphro, that what is pleasing to the gods and what is holy were not two separate things. In that case if holiness were loved because it was holy, then also what was pleasing to the gods would be loved because it pleased them; and, on the other hand, if what was pleasing to them pleased because they loved it, then also the holy would be holy because they loved it. But now you see that it is just the opposite, because the two are absolutely different from each other; for the one [what is pleasing to the gods] is of a sort to be loved because it is loved, whereas the other [what is holy] is loved because it is of a sort to be loved. Consequently, Euthyphro, it looks as if you had not given me my answer; as if when you were asked to tell the nature of the holy, you did not wish to explain the essence of it; you merely tell an attribute of it, namely, that it appertains to holiness to be loved by all the gods. What it *is,* as yet you have not said. So, if you please, do not conceal this from me; no, begin again. Say what the holy is, and never mind if gods do love it, nor if it has some other attribute; on that we shall not split. Come, speak out. Explain the nature of the holy and unholy.

EUTHYPHRO. Now, Socrates, I simply don't know how to tell you what I think. Somehow everything that we put forward keeps moving about us in a circle, and nothing will stay where we put it.

SOCRATES. Your statements, Euthyphro, look like the work of Daedalus, founder of my line. If I had made them, and they were my positions, no doubt you would poke fun at me, and say that, being in his line, the figures I construct in words run off, as did his statues, and will not stay where they are put. Meanwhile, since they are your definitions, we need some other jest; for in fact, as you see yourself, they will not stand still.

EUTHYPHRO. But, Socrates, it seems to me that the jest is quite to the point. This tendency in our statements to go in a circle, and not to stay in one place, it is not I who put it there. To my mind, it is you who are the Daedalus; so far as I am concerned, they would have held their place.

SOCRATES. If so, my friend, I must be more expert in his art than he, in that he merely made his own works capable of moving, whereas I give this power not merely to my own, but, seemingly, to the works of other men as well. And the rarest thing about my talent is that I am an unwilling artist; since I would rather see our arguments stand fast and hold their ground than have the art of Daedalus plus all the wealth of Tantalus to boot. But enough of this. And since, to my mind, you are languid, I will myself make bold with you to show how you might teach me about holiness. Do not weaken. See if you do not think that of necessity all that is holy is just.

EUTHYPHRO. Yes, I do.

SOCRATES. Well then, is all justice holy too? Or, granted that all holiness is just, is justice not all holy, but some part of it is holy, and some part of it is not?

EUTHYPHRO. I do not follow, Socrates.

SOCRATES. And yet you surpass me in your wisdom not less than by your youth. I repeat, you are languid through your affluence in wisdom. Come, lucky friend, exert yourself! What I have to say is not so hard to grasp. I mean the very opposite of what the poet [Stasinus] wrote:

Zeus, who brought that all to pass, and made it all to grow,
You will not name; for where fear is, there too is reverence.

On that I differ from the poet. Shall I tell you why?

EUTHYPHRO. By all means.

SOCRATES. I do not think that 'where fear is, there too is reverence'; for it seems to me that there are many who fear sickness, poverty, and all the like, and so are afraid, but have no reverence whatever for the things they are afraid of. Does it not seem so to you?

EUTHYPHRO. Yes, certainly.

SOCRATES. Where, however, you have reverence, there you have fear as well. Is there anybody who has reverence and a sense of shame about an act, and does not at the same time dread and fear an evil reputation?

EUTHYPHRO. Yes, he will be afraid of it.

SOCRATES. So it is not right to say that 'where fear is, there too is reverence.' No, you may say that where reverence is, there too is fear; not, however, that where fear is, there always you have reverence. Fear, I think, is wider in extent than reverence. Reverence is a part of fear, as the uneven is a part of number; thus you do not have the odd wherever you have number, but where you have the odd you must have number. I take it you are following me now?

EUTHYPHRO. Yes, indeed.

SOCRATES. Well then, what I asked you was like that. I asked you if wherever justice is, there is holiness as well; or, granted that wherever there is holiness, there is justice too, if where justice is, the holy is not always to be found. Thus holiness would be a part of justice. Shall we say so, or have you a different view?

EUTHYPHRO. No, that is my opinion; I think that you are clearly right.

SOCRATES. Then see what follows. If holiness is a part of justice, it seems to me that we must find out what part of justice it is. Suppose, for instance, in our case just now, you had asked me what part of number is the even, and which the even number is; I would have said it is the one that corresponds to the isosceles, and not to the scalene. Does it not seem so to you?

EUTHYPHRO. It does.

SOCRATES. Then try to show me in this way what part of the just is holiness, so that we may tell Meletus to cease from wronging me, and to give up prosecuting me for irreligion, because we have adequately learned from you of piety and holiness, and the reverse.

EUTHYPHRO. Well then, Socrates, I think that the part of justice which is religious and is holy is the part that has to do with the service of the gods; the remainder is the part of justice that has to do with the service of mankind.

SOCRATES. And what you say there, Euthyphro, to me seems excellent. There is one little point, however, on which I need more light. I am not yet quite clear about the thing which you call 'service.' I suppose you do not mean the sort of care we give to other things. The 'service' of the gods is not like that—the sort of thing we have in mind when we assert that it is not everybody who knows how to care for horses. It is the horseman that knows, is it not?

EUTHYPHRO. Yes, certainly.

SOCRATES. I suppose it is the special care that appertains to horses?

EUTHYPHRO. Yes.

SOCRATES. In the same way, it is not every one who knows about the care of dogs; it is the huntsman.

EUTHYPHRO. True.

SOCRATES. The art of the huntsman is the care of dogs.

EUTHYPHRO. Yes.

SOCRATES. And that of the herdsman is the care of cattle.

EUTHYPHRO. Yes, certainly.

SOCRATES. And in the same way, Euthyphro, holiness and piety mean caring for the gods? Do you say so?

EUTHYPHRO. I do.

SOCRATES. And so the aim of all this care and service is the same? I mean it thus. The care is given for the good and welfare of the object that is served. You see, for instance, how the horses that are cared for by the horseman's art are benefited and made better. Don't you think so?

EUTHYPHRO. Yes, I do.

SOCRATES. And so no doubt the dogs by the art of the huntsman, the cattle by that of the herdsman, and in like manner all the rest. Unless, perhaps, you think that the care may tend to injure the object that is cared for?

EUTHYPHRO. By Heaven, not I!

SOCRATES. The care aims at its benefit?

EUTHYPHRO. Most certainly.

SOCRATES. Then holiness, which is the service of the gods, must likewise aim to benefit the gods and make them better? Are you prepared to say that when you do a holy thing you make some deity better?

EUTHYPHRO. By Heaven, not I!

SOCRATES. Nor do I fancy, Euthyphro, that you mean it so; far from it. No, it was on this account that I asked just what you meant by service of the gods, supposing that, in fact, you did not mean that sort of care.

EUTHYPHRO. And, Socrates, you were right. I do not mean it so.

SOCRATES. Good. And now what kind of service of the gods will holiness be?

EUTHYPHRO. Socrates, it is the kind that slaves give to their masters.

SOCRATES. I understand. It seems to be a kind of waiting on the gods.

EUTHYPHRO. Just that.

SOCRATES. See if you can tell me this. The art which serves physicians, what result does it serve to produce? Don't you think that it is health?

EUTHYPHRO. I do.

SOCRATES. Further, what about the art that serves the shipwrights? What result does it serve to produce?

EUTHYPHRO. Obviously, Socrates, the making of a ship.

SOCRATES. And that which serves the builders serves the building of a house?

EUTHYPHRO. Yes.

SOCRATES. Now tell me, best of friends, about the service of the gods. What result will this art serve to produce? You obviously know, since you profess to be the best-informed among mankind on things divine!

EUTHYPHRO. Yes, Socrates, I say so, and I tell the truth.

SOCRATES. Then tell me, I adjure you, what is that supreme result which the gods produce when they employ our services?

EUTHYPHRO. They do many things and noble, Socrates.

14 SOCRATES. Just as the generals do, my friend. All the same you would have no trouble in summing up what they produce, by saying it is victory in war. Is n't it so?

EUTHYPHRO. Of course.

SOCRATES. And the farmers too, I take it, produce many fine results, but the net result of their production is the food they get from the earth.

EUTHYPHRO. Yes, surely.

SOCRATES. Well now, of the many fine and noble things which the gods produce, what is the sum of their production?

EUTHYPHRO. Just a little while ago I told you, Socrates, that the task is not a light one to learn precisely how all these matters stand. I will, however, simply tell you this. If any one knows how to say and do things pleasing to the gods in prayer and sacrifice, that is holiness, and such behavior saves the family in private life together with the common interests of the State. To do the opposite of things pleasing to the gods is impious, and this it is that upsets all and ruins everything.

SOCRATES. Surely, Euthyphro, if you had wished, you could have summed up what I asked for much more briefly. But the fact is that you are not eager to instruct me. That is clear. But a moment since, you were on the very point of telling me—and you slipped away. Had you given the answer, I would now have learnt from you what holiness is, and would be content. As it is—for perforce the lover must follow the loved one wherever he leads the way— once more, how do you define the holy, and what is holiness? Do n't you say that it is a science of sacrifice and prayer?

EUTHYPHRO. I do.

SOCRATES. Well, and is not sacrifice a giving to the gods, and prayer an asking them to give?

EUTHYPHRO. Precisely, Socrates.

SOCRATES. By this reasoning, holiness would be the science of asking from the gods and giving to them.

EUTHYPHRO. Quite right, Socrates; you have caught my meaning perfectly.

SOCRATES. Yes, my friend, for I have my heart set on your wisdom, and give my mind to it, so that nothing you say shall be lost. No, tell me, what is this service to the gods? You say it is to ask of them and give to them?

EUTHYPHRO. I do.

SOCRATES. And hence to ask aright will be to ask them for those things of which we stand in need from them?

EUTHYPHRO. What else?

SOCRATES. And, on the other hand, to give aright will be to give them in return those things which they may need to receive from us? I take it there would be no art in offering any one a gift of something that he did not need.

EUTHYPHRO. True, Socrates.

SOCRATES. And therefore, Euthyphro, holiness will be a mutual art of commerce between gods and men.

EUTHYPHRO. An art of commerce, if you like to call it so.

SOCRATES. Well, I do not like it if it is not so. But tell me, what advantage could come to the gods from the gifts which they receive from us? Everybody sees what they give us. No good that we possess but is given by them. What advantage can they gain by what they get from us? Have we so much the better of them in this commerce that we get all good things from them, and they get nothing from us?

EUTHYPHRO. What! Socrates. Do you suppose that the gods gain anything by what they get from us?

SOCRATES. If not, then what would be the meaning, Euthyphro, of these gifts to the gods from us?

EUTHYPHRO. What do you think they ought to mean but worship, honor, and, as I just now said, good will?

SOCRATES. So, Euthyphro, the holy is what pleases them, not what is useful to them, nor yet what the gods love?

EUTHYPHRO. I believe that what gives them pleasure is precisely what they love.

SOCRATES. And so once more, apparently the holy is that which the gods love.

EUTHYPHRO. Most certainly.

SOCRATES. After that, will you be amazed to find your statements walking off, and not staying where you put them? And will you accuse me as the Daedalus who makes them move, when you are yourself far more expert than Daedalus, and make them go round in a circle? Don't you see that our argument has come full circle to the point where it began? Surely you have not forgotten how in what was said before we found that holiness and what is pleasing to the gods were not the same, but different from each other. Do you not remember?

EUTHYPHRO. I do.

SOCRATES. And are you not aware now that you say that what the gods love is holy? But is not what the gods love just the same as what is pleasing to the gods?

EUTHYPHRO. Yes, certainly.

SOCRATES. Well then, either we were wrong in our recent conclusion, or if that was right, our position now is wrong.

EUTHYPHRO. So it seems.

SOCRATES. And so we must go back again, and start from the beginning to find out what the holy is. As for me, I never will give up until I know. Ah! do not spurn me, but give your mind with all your might now at length to tell me the absolute truth; for if anybody knows, of all mankind, it is you, and one must not let go of you, you Proteus, until you tell. If you did not know precisely what is holy and unholy, it is unthinkable that for a simple hireling you ever would have moved to prosecute your aged sire on a charge of murder. No, you would have feared to risk the wrath of the gods on the chance that you were not doing right, and would have been afraid of the talk of men. But now I am sure that you think you know exactly what is holy and what is not. So tell me, peerless Euthyphro, and do not hide from me what you judge it to be.

EUTHYPHRO. Another time, then, Socrates, for I am in a hurry, and must be off this minute.

SOCRATES. What are you doing, my friend? Will you leave, and dash me down from the mighty expectation I had of learning from you what is holy and what is not, and so escaping from Meletus' indictment? I counted upon showing him that now I had gained wisdom about things divine from Euthyphro, and no longer out 16 of ignorance made rash assertions and forged innovations with regard to them, but would lead a better life in future.

Apology

Apology

Though we do well to call this dialogue the Defence of Socrates, we may conveniently refer to it by its customary title of *Apology*. So Sir Philip Sidney, drawing arguments from Plato himself, meets the attack of the Platonic Socrates on mimetic art in a work which is known indifferently as *The Defence of Poesie* or *An Apology for Poetrie*. So Cardinal Newman, defending the course of his life, entitles his book *Apologia pro Vita Sua,* using the Latin (and Greek) word in order to avoid the risk of readers who might think that his change of cult demanded an apology in the common English sense.

Aristotle in the *Rhetoric* properly divides all speeches into three classes, each of them having two subdivisions. There are deliberative speeches, of counsel for or against, speeches of exhortation or dissuasion. There are speeches, again, of praise or blame, two subdivisions together forming the class called 'epideictic.' And there are speeches of accusation or defence. We use all six of these kinds of speaking in our daily life as well as on set occasions. And they constantly overlap. We can hardly accuse without blaming, or defend without praise, or praise or blame without exhorting or dissuading. This interwoven texture of speech occurs also in public speaking, though here a given utterance is more likely to show the predominant traits of one single species. In a trial or law-suit one man will give a speech of accusation (prosecution), the other a speech of defence.

In this dialogue of Plato, Socrates is made to give a speech of defence, which is supposed to begin soon after the last of two or more speeches of accusation—how many is not made clear. In opening, Socrates refers to 'my accusers.' Later it would seem that the last and main attacking speech was delivered by Meletus, and it is Meletus whom Socrates cross-examines in the passage which brings this work of Plato out of the realm of forensic oratory into dialogue. Two other accusers, Anytus and Lycon, are named along with Meletus; it is not clear that Anytus ever spoke against Socrates in public; and if Lycon spoke, there is no definite hint

43

of what he said. The last two divisions of Socrates' Apologia have in them definite elements both of counsel and of praise and blame.

For a beginning, Plato and his Socrates artistically burst into the midst of things. And the reference to 'my accusers' lets the speech bring in 'old' accusers along with these new ones; the distinction between old and recent witnesses is one that Aristotle later found helpful in the *Rhetoric*. In the *Apology* the old include and specify Aristophanes in the *Clouds*, even by name, where Socrates is represented as a Sophist, and the chief of them, but surely for fun, and not, as some suppose, for the ends of bitter ridicule. There is great beauty in the *Clouds* as well as fun. However, it is true that every item in the charge of Meletus has its counterpart in the play, where we find the school of Socrates corrupting a young man, teaching how to make the worse appear the better reason, investigating things above the earth and underneath it, and bringing in new deities to replace the recognized gods of the State. By reference to the play, the dialogue makes clear the division between the 'old' and Meletus the 'new,' and also the relation between them. But the reference provokes a smile, and the smile is in keeping with Plato's aim, which we have noticed, of arousing the mingled emotions of laughter and tears. Meanwhile we must not forget that other poets besides Aristophanes had formerly made use of Socrates in comedy, among them Ameipsias in his *Connos* (the name of Socrates' music-teacher); that the aim of these poets was hilarity and merry-making, not painful attack; and that Socrates in the *Clouds* is hardly worse handled than is Aeschylus in the *Frogs*, though many readers fail to see that Aristophanes is getting all the amusement he can out of Aeschylus and Euripides alike.

One other end is served when Socrates describes his ludicrous appearance in the *Clouds*, the end which Plato frequently has of making his hero ironic. We may add that Plato himself in his time suffered from the attention of the later comic poets, without, so far as we know, exhibiting any great rancor against them.

On the vexed and thorny question how far the dialogue is historical, and how far imaginative composition, we had best say not too much. The speech which Plato represents is one he heard, for he was present at the trial; and his fine memory, quite apart from the indelible impression which the trial and death of the master would make on a loved and loving pupil, could retain innumerable details for later use.

On the other hand, the *Apology* is a finished work of art, produced by the skilful hand of one who had already written dialogues, Socratic conversations, doubtless plenty of them; this work is not the sort of thing a man would write when his grief was fresh. Rather, it represents what Wordsworth calls 'emotion recollected in tranquility.' We have seen, too (p. 6), that the Socratic conversation as a literary species was in existence before Plato essayed it; and the spirit of art was strong in the men of his day. When Thucydides as a historian came to write the funeral oration of Pericles over the young men dead in the war, he had no speech before him, and composed the right one from his own historical imagination.

The main march of the *Apology*, and its division into one main section and two smaller ones, we may take to be historical. Some omission of redundant words and the like we may assume. The perfect verbal transitions and smooth advance from item to item, beneath the surface of apparent casual naturalness, all that can be done to turn nature into art —somewhat more than a speaker does in revising his own composition— we may probably attribute to Plato. We must not forget him, as so many readers do, for he is present all the time in the *Apology*. We cannot be sure just what Socrates said at his trial, but we know that the consummate artist wrote this dialogue. In reading it, do not forget Plato! Perhaps the last word on this question may be drawn from Aristotle and his *Poetics*; for the eloquent defence we here discuss is poetry. It is clear, thinks Aristotle (chapter 9), that sometimes history does possess the universal truth that makes a poem, and when a writer takes that piece of history and represents it in its universal truth, he is its 'poet.'

Plato, then, is both historian and poet. He gives us a lively picture of things as they were, and of a speech that was uttered by a man defending life and reputation. He gives us also a universal defence of the philosophic or scholarly life; for we may keep reminding ourselves that philosophy does not mean for Plato simply what we commonly mean by 'metaphysics.' We realize better what philosophy means to him when we take the word to pieces, and see that it must mean the love of wisdom and of learning in the widest sense, of learning in mathematics, literature, and law, as well as physics. Of course that means the highest wisdom which rises out of and above all special forms of learning. As the book of Aristotle which we call the *Metaphysics* shows, philosophy means a love of the study of causes, the first cause, and God. The *Apology* defends the life of contemplation; pure contemplation, reaching from things earthly to the highest, but not an activity engaged in by a mind that never studied books or consorted with the gifted and instructed of every sort, never learned from the best of books and of men.

The dialogues *Crito* and *Phaedo* continue the defence. They will speak for themselves; here we may note, however, one characterization of the philosophic life that is offered, not by the *Apology*, but by *Phaedo*: philosophy, the way of Socrates' life as he lived it, is the practice of music.[1]

So the *Apologia pro Vita Sua* which Plato puts into the mouth of Socrates is a defence of Plato's way of living too, and of the scholarly and philosophic life whenever and wherever it is lived in obedience to God for the glory of God, for the happiness of him who lives it, and for the welfare of the State.

The *Apology* defends the life of the mind. It also stirs the emotions. And because of its emotional appeal it is often called a tragedy. The division into episodes or acts, the suspense throughout, but especially between the first and the second episode, the action as a whole, serious, complete, of magnitude, arousing emotions like fear and pity, or akin to them; these elements and aspects all allow us to call the work a tragedy if we use the word in a looser sense. Nor is there any question that in writing the work Plato felt the influence of the Greek tragic drama. Further, we again recall the story that in youth he practised writing dramas, and destroyed them when he joined the group of Socrates. There is in the Socrates of the *Apology* something like a tragic flaw; we are made to feel that with a little care, and with no sacrifice of principle, the hero might have won the votes of the majority, and so saved his life. But Socrates, as Plato represents him, does not taunt his judges—as Antigone taunts Creon, and infuriates him with an accusation, when the business of her speech of defence was to save her life, and save herself for her betrothed. The *Apology* does not display a flaw of character, defect of judgment, or serious mistake, of the sort that plunges a man or his family in a drama from happiness into utter misery. The character of Socrates is, rather, somewhat like that of a Christian martyr; and though emotions like fear and pity are aroused in us by the complication and solution so concretely represented to us, these emotions are not the fear and pity of a tragic drama, and they are enveloped by a sense of exultation or exaltation rather than grief.

The *Apology* could, however, be staged; the effect would be very dramatic; the situation, which is that of the court, and not a theatre, would thus come out the more effectively. The scene could then be compared with the great trial-scene devised by Aeschylus in the *Eumenides*. Too many have compared the trial of Socrates with that of Christ. It

1 *Phaedo* 61 a; see below, p. 115.

does not produce the exaltation of the Mass. And, finally, we must re-mark that the *Apology* is not a drama but a dialogue.

In it, we may, before closing, note two matters more of some im-portance. First we may observe how Plato in dealing with the trial and death of Socrates makes him swear by the accredited gods of the State. This point may be noted in all four dialogues about that trial and its outcome, but seems to be of special interest in the *Apology* where Socra-tes defends himself against the charge of atheism, and of not believing in the recognized gods. True, he swears once (22 a) 'by the Dog,' his own customary and familiar oath; compare the Prioress of Chaucer in the Prologue to the *Canterbury Tales:* 'Her greatest oath was by Saint Loy.' For Socrates there probably is nothing in an oath by the Egyptian dog-faced god that supposedly would annoy the audience at Athens. But his quest of a person wiser than himself was undertaken, so he argues, in obedience to the will of the god at Delphi, which meant Apollo. This theme runs through and dominates the dialogue. In his colloquy with Meletus, he swears (24 e) 'by Hera,' and adjures his foe to answer (25 c), 'in the name of Zeus'; and again (26 b), 'in the name of those very gods we are discussing'; and once more (26 e) 'before Zeus' (translated, p. 60, 'by Heaven').

As for the quest, it is a highly useful and amusing device for gaining interest. I wonder why more use has not been made of it by writers in all ages; or the present reference may serve to recall more instances of its use than I happen to know. It is not the quest of the Golden Fleece or the quest of the Holy Grail, or that of a traveler in search of the pic-turesque, or in search of an undiscovered route or land, or even of Coelebs in search of a wife. There are many interesting quests like that. But this is the quest of a man for a kind of man. In the time of Plato we hear about one other quest of this description, the search of Diogenes with his lamp for a 'man'—presumably a *real* one; the modern version has Diogenes going about by daylight with a lantern looking for an 'honest' man; it is the nearest parallel to Socrates' unending search for a wise one. I can think of but two other cases. Van Leeuwenhoek, the father of bacteriology, on finding microscopic organisms in his own saliva, was told by his critics that he found them there because he drank beer; whereupon, the story goes, he set out with his lenses upon a search for a man in all the Netherlands who drank no beer. The story differs from the tales of Socrates and the Cynic. Diogenes never found an honest man, nor Socrates a wiser than himself who knew that he knew nothing.

Van Leeuwenhoek after an almost endless search did find a man who drank no beer, and whose mouth contained microbes.

The fourth case is my own. All the good scholars I have known or read about, including Socrates and Plato, and Aristotle too, could teach; the better the scholar, the better the teacher, having better things to give, and being the more eager to impart them. Yet for forty years I have heard that there are learned scholars who cannot teach. That must mean a man who can teach nobody but himself, else how could he be learned? Well, as Socrates might say, I have searched for this real scholar, one neither deaf nor dumb, who can teach nobody but himself. And I have not found him. Pedants there are enow. But a pedant is not a scholar. Above all, in addition to some learning, and some knowledge of tongues, a teacher has—must have, as Paul warns us, or be 'nothing'—he must have love. Paul does not say that languages are futile when they perform their function, or that knowledge is nothing if you mingle with it something else, namely love. Yet people go on talking of the animal in question, this truly learned man who cannot teach, and the scholar goes on searching for him, never finding; for the truth is, fellow citizens, that a man who cannot teach another probably cannot teach himself, and really can be taught nothing that is much worth knowing.

Apology of Socrates

What effect my accusers had upon you, Men of Athens, 17
I know not. As for me, they well-nigh made me forget who I was,
so telling were their speeches! And yet, so to say, not one atom of
truth did they utter. But that which astonished me most among
all their fabrications was this, that they said you must be on your
guard, and not be deceived by me, as I was a masterly speaker.
That they should not be ashamed when they were promptly going
to be caught by me in a lie, through the fact, since I shall show
myself to be no orator at all, therein methought they reached the
very height of their effrontery; unless perchance what they call
masterly speaker means the one who tells the truth. If that is what
they are saying, then I will admit I am an orator, though not of the
sort they describe.

Well then, as I say, these men have uttered nothing, or next to
nothing, that is true. From me, however, you shall hear the simple
truth. But, by Heaven! fellow citizens, it will not be in language
like theirs, decked out with epithets and phrases, nor beautifully
ordered; rather you shall hear such utterances as come to me, in
any words that offer, for of the justice of what I say I am convinced,
and from me you need none of you expect aught else. No, Gentlemen! it would hardly befit a man of my age to come into your
presence moulding phrases like a youngster. And nevertheless,
my fellow citizens, and above all, I do request and beg of you this
thing: if you should hear me pleading my cause with the same
expressions I habitually have used in speaking, whether at the
market by the counters, where many of you have heard me, or
elsewhere, do not for that reason marvel and make a disturbance.
The facts stand thus. At the age of seventy years I now for the

first time have come up before a tribunal, and so I am an absolute stranger to the language of this place. Let it be as if I really were a foreigner here, since then you surely would excuse me if I used the accent and manner of speech in which I was reared. And so I now make this request of you, a matter of justice as it seems to me, that you let me use my way of speaking; it may be better, it may be worse, but the only thing you have to consider is this, and this is what you have to put your mind on, whether that which I say is right or not. That is the merit of a judge; the merit of a speaker is to tell the truth.

To begin with, fellow citizens, it is right for me to answer the earliest charges falsely brought against me, and my first accusers, and then I must answer the charges and accusers that come later.

Many, in fact, were they who formerly brought charges against me, yes many years ago, and spoke not a word of truth. And them I fear more than I do the group of Anytus, dangerous as these are too. No, Gentlemen, those others are more dangerous, for they have prejudiced the major part of you since your childhood, convincing you of an utterly false charge against me; to wit, 'There is a person, Socrates by name, a "wise man," who speculates about the heavens above, and also searches into everything below the earth, and in argument can make the worse case win.' [2] Those persons who have spread this charge abroad, they, fellow citizens, are my dangerous accusers; for people who listen to them think that men who make the said investigations do not believe in any gods. Add that these accusers are many in number, have brought their charges for a long time now, and, moreover, made them to you when you most readily believed things, when some of you were children or striplings; sheer accusation of an absent person without anybody to defend him. And what is most baffling of all, it is impossible to identify and name them, unless perchance in the case of a certain comic poet. For the rest, for all who through jealousy and malice misled you, and those who, once they were misled, got others to believe the same—with all these it is impossible to deal. There is no means of bringing one of them here to

[2] The proverbial translation is: 'To make the worse appear the better reason.'

court, or putting a single one to cross-examination. No, in making my defence I am simply forced to fight, as it were, with shadows, and to question with nobody to make reply. Accordingly, I ask you to assume with me that, as I say, my accusers fall into these two classes, one group who are accusing me at present, the other those who of old accused me as aforesaid; and understand that it is these I must reply to first, for it is they whom you heard bringing charges earlier, and far more than this group who now come after.

Well then, fellow citizens, I must now make my defence, and must try to clear away in this brief time that calumny which you have entertained so long. I would that this might come to pass, if so it should be better for both you and me, and if it profits me to plead. But I think the task to be a hard one, and what its nature is I am by no means unaware. Still, let the outcome be as it pleases God; the law must be obeyed, and the defence be made.

Let us, then, go back and look at the original accusation from which the slander arose, the slander that gave Meletus his ground for this indictment he has lodged against me. Let us see. Precisely what did the slanderers say when they slandered? We must read their complaint as if it were a legal accusation: 'Socrates is wicked; overdoes inquiry into what occurs below the earth and in the heavens; in arguing makes the worse case win; and teaches others to do the same as he.' Such is in substance the accusation—what you actually saw in the comedy [the *Clouds*] of Aristophanes, where a man called 'Socrates' is swung about, declaring that he treads the air, and sputtering a deal of other nonsense on matters of which I have not one bit of knowledge either great or small. And I do not say so in disparagement of any science such as that, if any one is learned in such matters; I should not wish to be attacked by Meletus upon so grave a charge. But actually, fellow citizens, to me these matters are of absolutely no concern. I call the greater part of you yourselves to witness, and beg all who ever heard me in discussion to tell one another and declare it; many of you are in a position to do this. Declare to one another, therefore, whether any of you ever heard me dealing with such matters either briefly or at length. In that way you will see what all the rest amounts to of what the generality of people say concerning me.

No, there is nothing in it whatsoever. And if you have heard anybody say that I profess to give instruction, and get money in that way, neither is that true; although to my mind it is very fine indeed if any one is able to instruct his fellows, as are Gorgias of Leontini, and Prodicus of Ceos, and Hippias of Elis. Each one of them is able, Gentlemen, to go to city after city and attract young men; youths who might without expense consort with any one they chose among their own fellow citizens, these they persuade to give up that fellowship, to consort with them, to pay them money, and to be grateful to them besides. And indeed there is another man of learning here, from Paros, who, I learned, was staying in the City, for I happened to be calling on a man, Callias son of Hipponicus, who has paid more money to the Sophists than have all the others put together. And so I questioned him, he having, in fact, two sons:

'Callias,' said I, 'if your two sons had been colts or calves, we should have no trouble in finding some one to look after them, who for pay would make them fine and good according to the standard of their kind. We should pick some trainer of horses, say, or farmer. But now that they are human beings, whom have you in mind to put in charge of them? Who is there with a knowledge of their proper quality, the excellence of a human being and a citizen? I fancy you have given thought to this since you have sons. Is there any one,' said I, 'or not?'

'Yes, certainly,' said he.

'Who?' said I. 'Whence comes he? What does he charge for teaching?'

'Socrates,' he said, 'it is Evenus; comes from Paros; charge, five minae.'

So I thought Evenus was a lucky man if he really had this art, and would teach it at so reasonable a rate. For myself, I should be very proud and self-conceited if I knew all that. But the truth is, fellow citizens, I have no such knowledge.

Then perhaps some one of you may be inclined to ask: 'But, Socrates, what *is* the matter with you? What is the origin of these charges that are made against you? Unless you acted very differently from everybody else, surely no such story and repute would have arisen—if you did not do something other than most people do. Tell us what it is, in order to keep us from rushing to our own conclusion about you.'

That, I take it, would be fairly spoken; and I shall try to show you what it is that has given me this name and ill repute. Pray listen. Some of you, perhaps, will take me to be joking, but be assured that I shall tell you the simple truth. The fact is, fellow citizens, that I have got this name through my possession of a certain wisdom. What sort of wisdom is it? A wisdom, doubtless, that appertains to man. With respect to this, perhaps, I actually am wise; whereas those others whom I just now mentioned may possibly be wise with a wisdom more than human, or else I do not know what to say of it; as for me, I certainly do not possess it, and whoever says I do is lying, and seeks to injure me.

And, fellow citizens, do not interrupt me even if I say what seems extravagant, for the statement I shall make is not my own; instead, I shall refer you to a witness whose word can be accepted. Your witness to my wisdom, if I have any, and to its nature, is the god at Delphi. You certainly knew Chaerephon. He was a friend of mine from our youth, and a friend of your popular party as well; he shared in your late exile, and accompanied you on your return. Now you know the temper of Chaerephon, how impulsive he was in everything he undertook. Well so it was when once he went to Delphi, and made bold to ask the oracle this question—and, Gentlemen, please do not make an uproar over what I say; he asked if there was any one more wise than I. Then the Pythian oracle made response that there was no one who was wiser. To this response his brother here will bear you witness, since Chaerephon himself is dead. .

Now bear in mind the reason why I tell you this. It is because I am going on to show you whence this calumny of me has sprung; for when I heard about the oracle, I communed within myself: 'What can the god be saying, and what does the riddle mean? Well I know in my own heart that I am without wisdom great or small.

What is it that he means, then, in declaring me to be most wise? It cannot be that he is lying; it is not in his nature.' For a long time I continued at a loss as to his meaning, then finally decided, much against my will, to seek it in the following way.

I went to one of those who pass for wise men, feeling sure that there if anywhere I could refute the answer, and explain to the oracle: 'Here is a man that is wiser than I, but you said I was the wisest.' The man I went to was one of our statesmen; his name I need not mention. Him I thoroughly examined, and from him, as I studied him and conversed with him, I gathered, fellow citizens, this impression. This man appeared to me to seem to be wise to others, and above all to himself, but not to be so. And then I tried to show him that he thought that he was wise, but was not. The result was that I gained his enmity and the enmity as well of many of those who were present. So, as I went away, I reasoned with myself: 'At all events I am wiser than this man is. It is quite possible that neither one of us knows anything fine and good. But this man fancies that he knows when he does not, while I, whereas I do not know, just so I do not fancy that I know. In this small item, then, at least, I seem to be wiser than he, in that I do not fancy that I know what I do not.' Thereafter I went to another man, one of those who passed for wiser than the first, and I got the same impression. Whereupon I gained his enmity as well as that of many more.

Thereafter I went from one man to another, perceiving, with grief and apprehension, that I was getting hated, but it seemed imperative to put the service of the god above all else. In my search for the meaning of the oracle I must go to all who were supposed to have some knowledge. And, fellow citizens, by the Dog, since I have to tell you the truth, here is pretty much what I encountered. The persons with the greatest reputation seemed to me to be the ones who were well-nigh the most deficient, as I made my search in keeping with the god's intent; whereas others of inferior reputation I found to be men superior in regard to their possession of the truth. I needs must tell you all about my wandering course, a veritable round of toils heroic, which I underwent to prove that the oracle was not to be refuted.

After the statesmen, I went to the poets, tragic, dithyrambic, and the rest. There, I thought, my ignorance would be self-evident in comparison with them. So I took those poems of theirs which seemed to me to have been most carefully wrought by them, and asked the authors what they meant, in order that I might at the same time learn from them. Well, Gentlemen, I am ashamed to tell you the truth; and yet it must be done. The fact is, pretty nearly everybody, so to say, who was present could have spoken better than the authors did about the poems they themselves had written. So here again in a short time I learned this about the poets too, that not by wisdom do they make what they compose, but by a gift of nature and an inspiration similar to that of the diviners and the oracles. These also utter many beautiful things, but understand not one of them. And such, I saw, was the experience of the poets. At the same time I perceived that their poetic gift led them to fancy that in all else, too, they were the wisest of mankind, when they were not. So I went away from them as well, believing that I had the same advantage over them as over the statesmen.

To make an end, I went, then, to the artisans. Conscious that I did not, so to say, know anything myself, I was certain I should find that they knew many things and fine. Nor in that was I deceived; they did indeed know things which I did not, and in that they were wiser than I. But, fellow citizens, these excellent workmen seemed to me to have the same defect as the poets. Because they were successful in the practice of their art, each thought himself most wise about all other things of the highest import, and this mistake of theirs beclouded all that wisdom. So I asked myself the question, for the oracle, whether I preferred to be just what I was, neither wise as they were wise nor ignorant as they were ignorant, or to be both wise and ignorant like them. And my response to myself and the oracle was that it paid me to be as I was.

Such, fellow citizens, was the quest which brought me so much enmity, hatreds so utterly harsh and hard to bear, whence 23 sprang so many calumnies, and this name that is given me of being 'wise'; for every time I caught another person in his ignorance, those present fancied that I knew what he did not. But, Gentlemen, in all likelihood it really is the god who is wise, and by that oracle he meant to say that human wisdom is of little worth, or none. And it appears that when he picked out 'Socrates,' he used my name to take me for an example; it was as if he said: 'O race of men, he is the wisest among you, who, like Socrates, knows that in truth his knowledge is worth nothing.' So even now I still go about in my search, and, in keeping with the god's intent, question anybody, citizen or stranger, whom I fancy to be wise. And when it seems to me that he is not, in defence of the god I show that he is not. And this activity has left me without leisure either to take any real part in civic affairs or to care for my own. Instead, I live in infinite poverty through my service to the god.

In addition, the young men who of their own accord are my companions, of the class who have most leisure, sons of the very rich—they listen with joy to the men who are examined; they often imitate me, and in turn attempt to test out others. And thereupon, I take it, they find a great abundance of men who imagine they have some knowledge, and yet know little or nothing. And then these men whom they examine get angry, not at them, but at me, and say there is one Socrates, a perfect blackguard, who corrupts the young. Yet when anybody asks them how he does it, and by teaching what, they have nothing to tell, nor do they know. But in order not to seem quite at a loss, they make the usual attacks that are leveled at philosophers, namely, about 'things occurring in the heavens and below the earth,' 'not believing in the gods,' and 'making the worse case win.' What they do not care to utter, I imagine, is the truth: that they have been shown up in their pretense to knowledge when they actually knew nothing. Accordingly, since they are proud, passionate, and numerous, and organized and effective in speaking about me, they have long since filled your ears with their violent calumnies.

From among them have come Meletus, Anytus, and Lycon to attack me; Meletus aggrieved on behalf of the poets, Anytus on behalf of the artists and the politicians, Lycon on behalf of the rhetoricians. Consequently, as I said at the beginning, I shall be surprised if I succeed, within so short a time, in ridding you of all this swollen mass of calumny.

There, fellow citizens, you have the truth. I hide nothing from you, either great or small, nor do I dissimulate. And yet I know that even by this I stir up hatred, which itself proves that I tell the truth, and that it is precisely this that constitutes the charge against me, and is the cause of it. And whether now or later you investigate the matter, you will find it to be so.

Therewith let me close my defence to you on the charges made against me by my first accusers. As for Meletus, that honest man and good friend of the City, as he styles himself, to him and my more recent foes I will now endeavor to reply.

Here again, since the present charges vary from the former, let us take the actual text of the complaint. It runs, in effect, as follows: 'Socrates,' it declares, 'offends against the law since he corrupts the young, does not believe in the gods the State believes in, and believes in novel deities [spirits, *daimonia*] instead.' Such is the accusation. Let us examine it point by point.

First, it holds that I offend by corrupting the young. But I, fellow citizens, I hold that Meletus offends in that he makes a jest of a serious matter, when he lightly brings men to trial on questions in which he pretends to be deeply interested and concerned, whereas he never took the slightest interest in any of them. That this is so, I will try to prove to you.

Your attention, Meletus! Answer! Do you not attach the utmost importance to the moral improvement of our youth?

[MELETUS.] I do indeed.

Well then, tell the assembly here, who makes the young men better? You obviously know, for it is your special concern. You have discovered, so you state, who it is that corrupts them: I, whom you bring hither and accuse. Come now, tell who the person is who makes them better, and name him to these judges.

See, Meletus, you are silent. Have you nothing to say? Does n't that seem shameful to you, and proof enough of my assertion that you have had no interest in the matter? But come, friend, say who makes them better?

[MELETUS.] The laws.

No, my good fellow, that is not what I ask. I mean, what man? for, obviously, first of all he will have to know this very thing, the laws.

[MELETUS.] These judges, Socrates.

What say you, Meletus? These judges here are competent to instruct the young, and make them better?

[MELETUS.] Most certainly.

All are able? Or some are, and some are not?

[MELETUS.] All of them!

By Hera, that is welcome news! We have an ample store of men who benefit their kind! What next? What about the audience here, do these too make them better?

25 [MELETUS.] Yes, they too.

What about the Council?

[MELETUS.] Yes, the Council also.

But, Meletus, what about the men in the Assembly, the members of it, do they corrupt the young, or do they one and all make young men better?

[MELETUS.] Yes, they do it too.

So it seems that every one in Athens except me makes them fine and good, and I alone corrupt them. Is that your meaning?

[MELETUS.] Precisely that.

You detect me in a most unlucky situation. Answer me, though. Does the same thing seem to you to hold for horses too? Do you think all other men make horses better, and only one man ruins them? Or is it just the opposite of this, that some one man, or a very few, the horsemen, can improve them, whereas most people, if they have to deal with horses, and to make use of them, will spoil them? Is that not so, Meletus, both with horses and all other animals? It surely is, whether Anytus and you deny it or admit it. And what wonderful luck it would be for the young people if there were only one who did them harm, and all others did them good! But no, Meletus, you give ample proof that you never cared

at all about the young; and your indifference is clearly shown—
that you had no interest whatever in the things for which you
bring me into court.

Now, Meletus, another question. In the name of Zeus, tell us
whether it is better to live with honest citizens or with bad ones.
Answer, friend; I ask you nothing difficult. Don't the wicked
always do some evil to their neighbors, and the good some good?

[MELETUS.] Certainly.

Well, is there anybody who would rather be harmed than helped
by those he lives with? Answer, my friend; the law requires you
to do so. Does anybody like to be injured?

[MELETUS.] Certainly not.

Come now. When you bring me into court for corrupting the
younger generation and making them worse, do you charge that
I do so purposely or without design?

[MELETUS.] Purposely, say I.

What's that, Meletus? Are you at your age so much wiser than
I am at mine? And thus, while you know that the wicked always
do some injury to their nearest neighbors, and the good some good,
I, you think, am come to such a state of ignorance as not to know
that if I make some one I live with bad, I run the risk of getting
injured by him? So according to you I do myself all this harm on
purpose! That, Meletus, you will not get me to believe, nor, I fancy,
anybody else in all the world. No, either I do not corrupt them, 26
or if I do corrupt them, it is not by design. So either way you lie.
If I ruin them unwittingly, the case is that of an involuntary error
which does not legally bring me before this court; the proper thing
would be to take me privately, and to instruct and warn me; for
obviously when I learn better I shall stop doing what I do unwittingly. But you avoided joining me in order to instruct me; you
chose not to do it. You bring me to this court where it is legal to try
those who stand in need of punishment, not of learning.

There, fellow citizens, you have evidence enough of what I said,
that Meletus has not taken the slightest interest in these matters.

Yet tell us, Meletus: in what way do you say I corrupt the
younger men? Or is it not clear from the text of your complaint

that you mean I teach them not to believe in the gods the State believes in, but in other new divinities? Isn't that the way you mean I corrupt them by my teaching?

[MELETUS.] Yes, that is just what I assert.

In that case, Meletus, in the name of those very gods we are discussing, explain your meaning still more clearly to these gentlemen here and me, for there is a point I am unable to make out. If you mean that I teach them to believe in the existence of certain gods, then I myself believe that there are gods, and so I am not out and out an atheist, and do not break the law in that respect. Or do you mean that they are not the gods the State believes in, but other gods instead, and is this the point of your complaint, that they are different? Or do you say that I myself do not believe in any gods at all, and that I teach this disbelief to others?

[MELETUS.] Yes, that is what I maintain, that you do not believe in any gods at all.

You amaze me, Meletus. How can you say so? Do you mean that I do not, like other men, regard the sun and moon as gods?

[MELETUS.] By Heaven, Gentlemen of the Jury, he does not; he holds that the sun is a stone, and the moon an earth.

You must think you are accusing Anaxagoras, my dear Meletus. Have you such a poor opinion of these men here, and do you think them so illiterate as not to know that the works of Anaxagoras of Clazomenae are full of these ideas? And so you think that the young men learn these things from me, when on occasion they could buy the books for a drachma at most in the orchestra, and then laugh at Socrates if he pretended that these theories were his—apart from the fact that they are so bizarre! But, by Heaven, is that the way you think of me, that I don't believe in any god whatever?

[MELETUS.] No, by Heaven, not a single one.

Now that, Meletus, is incredible, and something that I take it you do not believe yourself. In my opinion, fellow citizens, this man is an utterly overweening and unbridled person, who has brought this accusation simply out of insolence, intemperance, and youthful rashness. It looks as if he had made up a riddle with 27 which to try me out: 'See whether Socrates, the wise man, will know that I am jesting and self-contradictory, or whether I shall fool him and all the rest who listen'; for to me he clearly contradicts himself in the complaint, where in effect he says: 'Socrates offends by not believing in gods, but by believing in gods.' And that is simply joking.

Examine with me, Gentlemen, my way of showing that he says this. And, Meletus, you answer us. But, Gentlemen, remember the request I made at the outset, and do not interrupt if I pursue the argument in my customary fashion.

Is there any living man, Meletus, who believes that there are human things, but does not believe that there are human beings? Let him answer, Gentlemen, and not make noisy protests beside the point. Does any one believe in horsemanship, and not in horses? Or does any one believe there is an art of piping, but that there are no pipers? No, honorable sir, there is n't any one who does it. If you do not choose to answer, I will speak for you and these others here as well. But give the answer to this. Is there anybody who believes in the doings of spirits [*daimonia*], but thinks there are no spirits [*daimones*]?

[MELETUS.] No.

How you oblige me by the grudging answer these gentlemen force you to make! Well then, you admit, I believe and teach that there are doings of spirits, whether recent or of old. At all events I do believe in them according to your statement; you have even sworn to this in your complaint. But if I believe in them, then quite necessarily, I suppose, I must believe in spirits. Is n't it so? It must be. I put you down as in agreement since you make no reply.

Now, must we not consider spirits as either gods or the offspring of gods? Say yes or no.

[MELETUS.] Yes, certainly.

If, then, I think that there are spirits, as you assert, and if the spirits are in some way gods, am I not right in saying that you talk in riddles and are jesting? First you say that I do not believe in gods, and next that I do believe in them inasmuch as I believe in spirits. Or again: if the spirits [*daimones*] are illegitimate children of the gods, whether by nymphs or other mothers as report will have it, who on earth will ever think that there are children of the gods, but that there are no gods? It would be as queer as to think that mules were the offspring of horses and asses, but that horses and asses did not exist. No, Meletus, there is no way out of it; either you formulated this complaint in order to try us out, or else you could find no real crime with which to charge me. That you could get a living person with the least intelligence to admit that a given man believed in the doings of spirits but not of gods, and that the same man, again, believed in neither spirits, gods, nor heroes, is quite beyond the bounds of possibility.

No, fellow citizens, that I am guiltless with respect to Meletus' indictment seems to me to call for no long defence; rather, let this argument suffice. But what I have said before, that much antagonism has arisen against me in the minds of many, rest assured that it is true. And this it is that will undo me, if I am undone, not Meletus nor Anytus, but the slander of the many, and their malice. Many another man, and good ones, has it undone, and, methinks, it will yet undo. There is no danger that the thing may stop with me.

Perhaps some one will say: "Well, Socrates, aren't you ashamed that you pursued a course from which you now are in danger of death?' To that it would be right for me to reply: 'Good sir, it is not well said if you think that a man of any worth at all ought to calculate his chances of living or dying, and not rather look to this alone, when he acts, to see if what he does is right or wrong, and if his are the deeds of a good man or a bad. By your account, the demigods who fell at Troy would be sorry fellows, all of them, and notably the son of Thetis, who so despised all danger in comparison with any disgrace awaiting him, and with what result? When his mother saw him eager to slay Hector, she, the goddess, addressed him, as I recall, approximately thus: "My child, if you avenge the death of your comrade Patroclus by slaying Hector, then you yourself will die. For you the lot of death," she said, "comes straightway after Hector's." But he, on hearing that, made light of death and danger, fearing far more to live a coward and not avenge his loved ones. "Straightway let me die," said he, "once I give the villain his reward, and not continue here, a laughing-stock, beside the hollow ships, a burden to the earth." Do you think that he took heed of death or danger?'

That, fellow citizens, is the way things really stand. If any one is stationed where he thinks it is best for him to be, or where his commander has put him, there, as it seems to me, it is his duty to remain, no matter what the risk, heedless of death or any other peril in comparison with disgrace.

It would have been dreadful conduct, fellow citizens, had I acted otherwise. When the leaders you had chosen to command me assigned a post to me at Potidaea, at Amphipolis, and at Delium, in the face of death itself I was as steadfast as any one could be in holding the position where they placed me; and when the god, as I believed and understood, assigned to me as my duty that I should live the life of a philosopher, and examine myself and others, it would have been dreadful had I through fear of death, or of anything else whatever, deserted my post. Dreadful indeed would it be, and verily any one would then be justified in bringing me to trial for not believing in gods, when I had disobeyed the oracle, feared death, and thought that I was wise when I was not. 29

For, Gentlemen, to be afraid of death is nothing else than thinking that one is wise when one is not, since it means fancying that one knows what one does not. Nobody knows, in fact, what death is, nor whether to man it is not perchance the greatest of all blessings; yet people fear it as if they surely knew it to be the worst of evils. And what is this but the shameful ignorance of supposing that we know what we do not? It is there and in that perhaps that I differ, Gentlemen, from the majority of mankind; and if I might call myself more wise than another, it would be in this, that as I do not know enough about what goes on in Hades, so too I do not think that I know. But doing wrong, and disobeying the person who is better than myself, be it god or man, that I know is base and wicked. Therefore never for the sake of evils which I know to be such will I fear or flee from what for all I know may be a good.

Accordingly, suppose you were now to acquit me, and went against Anytus; he who says that either I ought not to have been summoned hither to begin with, or, once I appeared I must inevitably be put to death; for he tells you that, if I am freed, your sons, who already put in practice what Socrates teaches, will all be utterly ruined. Suppose with reference to that you were to say to me: 'Socrates, at present we shall not give Anytus our assent, but will acquit you, yet upon one condition, namely, that hereafter you shall not pass your time in this investigation nor pursue philosophy; if you are caught doing it again, you die.' Well, as I said, if you were ready to let me go upon these conditions, my reply to you would be:

'Fellow citizens, I respect and love you, but I must obey the god rather than you, and so long as I draw breath, and can pursue philosophy, I will not cease from it nor from exhorting you, and ever pointing out the way to any one of you I meet, saying to him as I have been wont: "Good friend, you are a citizen of Athens, the greatest of all cities and the most renowned for power and learning, and yet you feel no shame at giving your mind to money so that you may get as much as possible, and to your reputation and to honor; but for insight, for the truth, for your soul and how it shall be at its best, you do not care nor trouble." '

And if any one of you disputes it, and says that he does care, I shall not forthwith dismiss him and go away, but will question him, and sift him, and put him to the test; and if he seems to me to have no fund of virtue, while professing to have it, I shall reproach him with attaching little value to what has most importance, and taking paltry things for what is larger. So will I do with young and old, whatever he be that I meet with, foreigner or native, yet rather with you citizens since you are nearer to me by kin; for this, you may rest assured, is what the god demands of me. And I think that there never came to you a greater good in the City than the service I render the god.

All I do is to go about persuading you, both young and old, not to think first of your bodies or your property, nor to be so mightily concerned about them as about your souls, how the spirit shall be at its best; it is my task to tell you that virtue does not spring from wealth, but that wealth and every other good that comes to men in private life or in public proceed from virtue. If it is by saying this that I corrupt the young, then this must be injurious; but any one who holds that I say anything save this says nothing. On that head, fellow citizens, I may assure you that whether you trust Anytus or not, and whether you acquit me or do not acquit me, I shall not alter my course, no matter if I have to die a hundred times.

Now, fellow citizens, do not interrupt, but continue granting my request of you not to cry out at what I may say, but to listen; I do believe that you will profit if you listen. I am, in fact, about to tell you certain other things at which you might possibly protest. Yet please do not. No; for you may rest assured that if you condemn me to death, I being such a person as I say, you will do yourselves more harm than you do to me. As for me, Meletus will no more hurt me than will Anytus. It does not lie in his power, for in my belief the eternal order does not permit a better man to be harmed by a worse. Oh yes! quite possibly he might kill or banish me, or rob me of my civic rights; and doubtless this man and the next will think that these are major evils. I do not think them such; no, I think it a far greater evil for a man to do what this man now is doing, namely trying to get a man condemned to death unjustly.

So, fellow citizens, at present I am far from making my defence upon my own account, as one might think; I make it for your sake, in order that you may not, by condemning me, do wrong about the gift of the god to you; for if you have me put to death, you will not easily find another of the sort, fastened upon the City by the god, for all the world (if I may use a rather ludicrous comparison) like a gadfly on a great and noble horse that is somewhat sluggish on account of his size and needs the fly to wake him up. So, it seems to me, the god has fastened me like that upon the City, to rouse, exhort, and rebuke each one of you, everywhere besetting you, and never once ceasing all day long. Another one like that, Gentlemen, 31 you will not come by so easily; but if you listen to me, you will take good care of me. You may, however, quite possibly be annoyed like people awakened from their slumbers, and, striking out at me, may listen readily to Anytus and condemn me to death. Then you would finish out the rest of your life in sleep, unless the god were in mercy to send you some one else to take my place. That it is the deity by whom I, such as I am, have been given to the City you may see from this: it is not like human nature for me to neglect all my own concerns, to put up with a neglected household all these years, and to attend to your affair, ever going to you individually in private, like a father or an elder brother, urging you to care for your moral welfare. And if I got any profit from it all, if these exhortations brought me any pay, there would seem to be some reason in my conduct. As it is, you see for yourselves that my accusers, who, unashamed, have brought so many other charges against me, have yet not had the effrontery to present a witness to allege that I ever took any sort of fee or sought one. Why not? Because, methinks, the witness I present to show that I speak the truth is quite enough—my poverty.

Possibly it may look odd that I should busily go about in private with my counsels, but in public dare not approach the mass of you with counsel for the City. The reason for that is something you have often heard me speak of in many a place; it is that there comes to me a thing divine and spiritual, what Meletus has mockingly referred to in his indictment. From childhood on, this sign has come to me; it is a voice, which, when it comes, always deters me from what I am about to do, but never urges me to act. It is this that fights against my entering political affairs; and the opposition strikes me as being altogether good; for, fellow citizens, you may rest assured that if I, long ago, had tried to take up politics, I should long ago have perished, and been of no service whatever either to you or to myself. And do not be aggrieved at me for telling the truth: there is not a man on earth that is safe if he nobly puts himself in opposition to you or to any other crowd, and strives to stop all sorts of wrong and lawlessness in the State. But if any one is really going to battle for the right, and to be safe for some short time in doing it, he must perforce remain a private citizen; he must not appear in public life.

Of that I will furnish you with telling evidence, not arguments, but what you value, facts. Listen to what happened in my case, and you will see that I am not a man to yield to any one unjustly for fear of death, not even if by my not yielding I were at once to perish. The tale I shall tell you is of the legal sort and uninspiring, but is true.

I never held any public office, fellow citizens, but one: I was a member of the Council. And it happened that our tribe, Antiochis, had the executive function [*prytany*] at the time you wished to sentence in a body the ten commanders who failed to pick up the survivors of the naval action [at Arginusae]. The procedure was illegal, as after a while you all admitted. But at the time I was the only one of the prytanes who stood out against your doing an illegal act and voted against you; and although the orators were ready to indict me and arrest me, while you urged them on and made an uproar, I thought that I ought to risk all danger on the side of law and justice rather than side with you in an unjust decree for fear of imprisonment or death.

This took place while Athens still was a democracy. But again, when the oligarchy was established, the Thirty had me and four others summoned to the Rotunda, and ordered us to go get Leon of Salamis, and bring him thence to have him put to death; they gave such orders frequently to many other persons in order to involve as many as they could in their crimes. But there again I showed, by deeds, and not by words, that death, if I may speak quite baldly, meant nothing at all to me, while not to do an unjust or an impious act, this meant everything; for that power, however huge its sway, did not terrify me into doing what was wrong. No, when we came out of the Rotunda, the other four went off to Salamis and brought back Leon, and as for me I went to my home. And for that I might well have paid with my life, had the government not promptly fallen. Of these facts many persons will bear witness to you.

Well then, do you think I could have survived through all these years if I had taken part in state affairs, and, acting properly as a good citizen, had fought for justice, making this perforce of paramount importance? Far from it, fellow citizens; nor could any other living man have done it. As for me, all my life long, if ever I did anything in an official way, I showed myself to be that sort of 33 person, and in private just the same; never once did I yield to any one in any point against the right, not even to one of those whom my slanderers declare to be my pupils.

But I never have been anybody's teacher. If any one cares to listen to me as I speak and carry on my special function, be he young or old, I never have begrudged it. I am not one who will engage in discussion if he gets money, and if not refuses. No, rich and poor alike I am prepared to question, and whoever will may listen to what I say when I make reply. And for my part, if any of them turns out well or ill, I cannot rightly be held responsible when I never offered to give any one instruction, nor gave it. If any one asserts that he ever learned or heard a thing from me other than what all the others heard as well, rest assured that he who says so does not tell the truth.

Well then, why do certain persons like to spend so much of their time with me? I told you, fellow citizens, what the reason is. The truth of the matter is just what I said: they like to hear the sifting out of those who think that they are wise, but are not. The thing, in fact, is not unpleasant. But for me, as I aver, it is a task enjoined upon me by the deity, through oracles, through dreams, and in every single way that ever a divine injunction was laid upon a man to do a thing. These statements, fellow citizens, are true and are easily proved. Suppose I am at present ruining some of the young people, and already have perverted others; then necessarily, no doubt, a number of them, when they grew older, would have seen that on occasion, when they were young, I gave them evil advice, and would now appear in court to accuse and punish me. Or, if they themselves were unwilling to do it, then some of their relations, fathers, brothers, or others of their kin—if it were true that members of the family had received some injury from me—would now remember it, and have me punished. Certainly there are many of them present whom I see: first Crito here, a man of my own generation and my deme, father of yon Critobulus; next, Lysanias of Sphettus, father of yon Aeschines; add Antiphon here of Kephisia, father of Epigenes. Among others, men whose brothers have attended at the pastime, Nicostratus son of Theozotides and brother of Theodotus—as for Theodotus, he is dead, and therefore could not plead for me against him; so also Paralus here whose father is Demodocus and whose brother is Theages, Adei- 34 mantus son of Ariston whose brother is Plato here, and Aianto- dorus, whose brother is yon Apollodorus. And many others I could name to you, of whom Meletus surely ought to have offered some- body as witness in his accusation. If he forgot it then, let him present it now—I yield the point—and let him say if he has any evidence of the sort. But, Gentlemen, you will find the case to be the very opposite of that; will find them all prepared to help me, the ruiner, the man who has done injury to their kin, as Meletus and Anytus aver. The ruined themselves, of course, might have some reason for coming to my aid. But those who are not ruined, men already mature, the relatives of these, what other reason could they have for coming to my aid except the straight and just one, that they know that Meletus is lying, and that I am telling the truth?

There you have it, Gentlemen. That is pretty much what I might have to say in my defence, that with possibly some additions to the like effect. Perhaps, however, one or another of you will be angry when he recalls his own experience, in some trial he was engaged in of less gravity than this; if he besought and with many tears implored the judges, and, in order to arouse the greatest pity, brought in his children along with others of his kin and many friends; while, as for me, I shall do nothing of the sort, although I am in danger, as I might suppose, to the last degree of peril. Perhaps, then, as he thinks of this, he will bear himself with the less remorse towards me, and, irritated by these very things, will cast his vote in anger. Now if any of you feels so, though for my part I do not impute it—but if anybody feels that way, then it seems to me the proper thing for me to say to him would be: 'Good friend, I too have friends and relatives; in fact, my case is just as Homer says. "I did not spring from either oak or rock," but from mankind, and so I have a family and sons; three sons, my fellow citizens, one a youth, and the other two are little boys.' Neverthe- less not one of them will I bring hither imploring you to let me off. And why shall I do nothing of all that? Not, fellow citizens, out of hardihood, nor in disdain of you. And whether I fear death or not is another question; but for my own honor, and yours, and the honor of the entire City, it does not seem proper for me at my age, and with the name I have, to do any of these things. The opinion may be true, or may be false; at all events the view is held that Socrates is somehow different from the mass of men. Well, if those of you who are regarded as distinguished in point of wisdom, or of courage, or of any other quality, behaved like that, it would be shameful. And yet, often enough, I have seen persons of such sort, persons of some reputation, behaving in extraordinary fashion when they were to hear the verdict, as if they thought they must be going to suffer something terrible if they had to die—as if they thought that they would be immortal in case you did not condemn them. To my mind, they brought shame upon the City; anybody from another city would infer that the Athenians who were eminent for their virtue, those whom their fellows selected as their rulers and for other places of distinction, were in no way better than women. These things, fellow citizens, it behoves us not to do if we have any reputation whatsoever; and if we do them, you should not allow it. No; you should make this very thing quite clear, that you will far more readily give your vote against the person who drags in these tearful dramas, and makes the City ridiculous, than against the man who argues quietly.

But apart from the question of propriety, Gentlemen, it does not seem right to me to beg the judge for mercy, or, by doing it, to get away, when one ought rather to enlighten and convince him. He does not take his seat for this, the judge, to render justice as a favor, but to decide on what is just. Indeed he took an oath that he would not favor people according to his notion of them, but that he would give judgment in accordance with the laws. And so we should not get you into the habit of perjuring yourselves, nor should you get into it; neither of us should commit impiety. So do not ask me, fellow citizens, to treat you in a way which I take to be dishonorable, wrong, and impious; above all, by Zeus! when I am under accusation of impiety by this Meletus here present; for obviously, if I swayed you and by begging forced you to act against your oath, I would be teaching you not to believe that there are gods, and by my defence would simply accuse myself of not believing in them. But that be far from me! I do believe in them, my fellow citizens, as none of my accusers does; and to you I commend myself, and to the Deity, to judge concerning me what shall be best at once for me and for you.

[After the vote against him.]

If I am not distressed, my fellow citizens, at what has happened in that you voted to convict me, there are many reasons for it, and in particular that the outcome was to me not unexpected. What is to me far more surprising is the actual division of the votes. I thought for my part that the vote would go, not by this small majority, but by a large one. As it is, apparently, if only thirty votes had gone the other way, I should have been acquitted. Accordingly, so far as Meletus is concerned, it seems to me I do now stand acquitted, and not only that, but it must be clear to every one that if Anytus and Lycon had not come hither to accuse me, he would have had to pay one thousand drachmas as a fine for not obtaining a fifth part of the votes.

Meanwhile the man proposes for me the penalty of death. So be it. What penalty, fellow citizens, am I to offer you instead? Evidently what I ought to get? What is it, then? What do I deserve to get or pay? I who, when I had learned a thing, did not lead my life in peace, but neglecting what the many care for—wealth, household matters, military leadership and civic and the other high positions, coalitions, factions that arise in the State—thought myself in fact too good a man to enter into these affairs with safety. I did not enter there where if I came I was not to be of any use either to you or to myself, but going to you one by one in private, I did you, I aver, the greatest service possible. There I went trying to persuade each one of you not to care first for his own possessions before caring for himself and how he might be at his best and wisest, nor to set the affairs of the City above the

36

City itself, and to give attention to all other things in just that way. Being a man of that description, what ought I to get? Something good, my fellow citizens, if the award must truly square with the desert; and the good ought further to be something that fits my case. What, then, befits a poor man, a benefactor, who needs leisure for the office of exhorting you? Nothing is so proper as the maintenance of such a man in the Prytaneum, a reward far more befitting him than for any one of you who may have won a victory at Olympia with a horse or a pair of them or four. He makes you think that you are happy; I cause you to be so. He, moreover, has no need of maintenance; I stand in need of it. And so if I must get what I deserve, there is my proposal: maintenance in the Prytaneum.

37

Perhaps when I say that to you, you will think that I am talking with the same bravado as about the tears and supplications. It is not, fellow citizens, as you think; no, it is more like this. I am persuaded that I never willingly wronged any man, but I have not persuaded you, since we have had small time to reach an understanding; whereas if the law with you were what it is with others, if a case involving the penalty of death could not be settled in a day, but took a number, I believe I would have won you over. As matters stand, it is not easy in a limited time to refute a mass of slanders.

Persuaded that I do no wrong to any one, I am far from ready to do injustice to myself, and will not say of myself that I merit some evil, and should allot myself that sort of penalty. In fear of what? For fear that otherwise I shall suffer the thing which Meletus proposes, that of which I say I know not whether it is good or evil? Instead of that ought I to choose one of the things that I know for certain to be ills, and penalize myself with that? Imprisonment? Why should I live in prison, a slave to a recurrent board of governors, the Eleven? Or say a fine, and to be jailed until I pay it? But that would be no different for me from what I just now mentioned, since I have no money to pay with. Well, suppose I offered to go into exile. Perhaps you would accept that. But truly, fellow citizens, the love of life must have a powerful hold on me, and make me heedless, if I cannot reason thus: You who are my fellow citizens could not endure my doings and discussions; no, they were too much for you, and so irritating that now you seek to be rid of them. Well, will others bear them easily? Far from it, fellow citizens. And what a fine existence that would be, for a man of my age to go away and live a wanderer and a waif driven from city to city; for well I know that wherever I went the young would listen to me just as they do here. And if I drove them off, they would get the older men's permission, and themselves expel me. And if I did not, their fathers and relations would expel me on the sons' account.

Well, perhaps some one will say: 'Why can't you go away from us, and then keep quiet, Socrates, and live in peace?' But that is the thing that is hardest of all to make some of you see. If I say that this means disobedience to the god, and for that very reason I cannot keep still, you will not believe me, but will think I speak in irony. If, on the other hand, I say it is perhaps the greatest good that can befall a man, daily to argue about virtue, and to discuss the other subjects about which you have heard me debating and examining myself as well as others, if I add that for mankind the unexamined life is not worth living, still less will you believe me when I tell you that. These matters stand, however, Gentlemen, precisely as I say, only it is not easy to convince you. And meanwhile, for my part, I am not in the habit of thinking that I merit ill at all. If I had wealth, I would suggest a sum that I was in a position to pay, for in that case I should do myself no harm. But now the fact is that I haven't, unless you chose to set a fine for me at a rate that I could pay. Perhaps I could pay you a silver mina; so that is what I offer.

But Plato here, my fellow citizens, and Crito, Critobulus, and Apollodorus, bid me offer thirty minae upon their security. Well then, I offer that; these men will be adequate security to you for the amount.

38

[After he is condemned to death.]

For no great thrift in time, my fellow citizens, you will have from those who wish to vilify the City the name and blame of having put to death the wise man, Socrates; for they will call me wise, even if I am not, they who would defame you. If only you had waited for a little while, the thing would have occurred for you in the course of nature; for you can see my age, that I am far along in life, and near to death. I say this, not to all of you, but only to those who voted for my death. And to them I have also to say this as well. It may be, Gentlemen, that you think I lost my cause for lack of arguments of the sort with which I might have won you over, if I had thought that I ought to say and do all things in order to escape the verdict. Far from it. I lost for a lack, but not of arguments; it was for lack of impudence and daring, and for not being ready to say to you the sort of thing it would have given you most pleasure to hear—me weeping and wailing, and doing and saying any and every sort of thing that I hold to be unworthy of me, but you are accustomed to hear from the rest. No, I did not then believe that, to avoid a danger, I ought to do anything unseemly in a freeman, nor do I now regret my manner of defence. No, far rather would I choose this manner of defence, and die, than follow that, and live. Whether in a court of justice or in war neither I nor any other man should seek by using every means conceivable to escape from death; for in battle you very often see that if you throw away your weapons and beg those who are pursuing you for mercy, you may get out of dying. Indeed, in every sort of danger there are various ways of winning through, if one is ready to do and say anything whatever. No, Gentlemen, that is not the hard thing, to escape from death; ah no, far harder is it to escape from sin, for sin is swifter than death. And so I, being old and slow, am overtaken by the slower enemy; while my accusers, who are strong and swift, have been caught by the swifter, namely wickedness. And so I now depart, by you condemned to pay the penalty of death; and they, by the truth convicted of a base injustice. And as I abide the payment, so do they. Who knows?

Perhaps it had to be so, and I think that things are as they ought to be.

Touching the future, I desire to make for you who voted to condemn me, a prediction; for I am at the point where men foresee the future best—when they are soon to die. Let me tell you then, you men who have condemned me, that after I am gone there will straightway come upon you a chastisement far heavier, by Zeus, than the death you have set for me. You have now done this in the belief that you have freed yourselves from giving any reckoning for your life; but I tell you the result will be the very opposite for you. There will be more inquisitors to sift you, men whom I now hold in check without your knowing it. And they will be more critical as they are younger, and will annoy you more; for if you think that by putting men to death you will prevent the slur from being cast at you that you do not live aright, you are in error. This way of getting freedom is neither very sure nor fine; no, the finest and readiest way is this, not to interfere with other people, but to render oneself as good a man as possible. There is the prophecy I make for you who voted to condemn me. And of them I take my leave.

With those of you who voted to acquit me I should be glad to talk about this thing that has occurred, while the magistrates are busy and it is not time for me to go to the place where I must die. So, Gentlemen, please wait with me as long as that. There is nothing to keep us from talking to each other as long as it is allowed. To you as to friends I wish to explain the real meaning of what has just happened to me. 40

Justices, for when I call you that I am naming you aright, the thing that has come to me is wonderful.

My customary warning, by the spirit, in previous times has always, up to now, come to me very often to oppose me, even when a matter was quite unimportant, if ever I was going to do something amiss. But to-day, as you yourselves have witnessed, that thing has happened to me which anybody might suppose, and which is considered, to be the uttermost of evils. Yet neither did the sign from god oppose me when I left my house this morning, nor at the point when I ascended here to the tribunal, nor in my speech at anything I was about to say; though often when I have been talking elsewhere it has stopped me in the middle of a speech. But to-day, with reference to the whole procedure, not once did it oppose me in a thing I did or said. What, then, do I take to be the cause of this? No doubt this thing that has happened to me is good, and it cannot be that our supposition is correct when any of us think that death is a misfortune. For me, the proof of this is telling: it cannot be but that the customary sign would have opposed me, if I had not been about to do a thing that was good.

Let us view in another way how ample are the grounds for our hope that death is a good. To be dead is one of two things. Either it is a sort of non-existence, and the dead man has no feeling about anything whatever, or else, as people say, the soul experiences a shift and a migration from here into another place. Now if there is no feeling, if death is like a sleep in which one does not even dream, what a wonderful gain it would be! I believe if a man were to take that night in which he slept so deeply that he did not have a single dream, and compared it with the other nights and days of his life; if he had to say, upon reflection, how many days and nights, all told, in his life, he had passed better and more sweetly than that night; I believe that every one, not merely any private citizen, but the Great King himself, would find them easy to count up in comparison with all the others. So if death is a sleep like that, I say it is a gain; for thus all time appears to be no more than a single night. If, on the other hand, death is like a journey from here to another place, and if what they say is true, that everybody who has died is there, then, Justices, what greater good than this could there be? If, on arriving in Hades, one could be freed from those who here pretend that they are Justices, and there find those who by report deal real justice, Minos, Rhadamanthus, Aaecus, and Triptolemus, and all the rest of the demigods who were just in their lives here, what a small thing would that journey seem! Or, again, to be with Orpheus and Musaeus, with Hesiod and Homer, what price would not any of you pay for that? I would gladly die repeatedly, if all that is true. To me it would be a wonderful way to pass my time, there where I could meet with Palamedes and with Ajax son of Telamon, and any one else among the ancients who died through an unjust decision. To compare my lot with theirs, methinks, would not be so unpleasant; and most important of all would be to go on sifting people there, as here, and finding out who is wise, and who thinks he is so, but is not. What would not anybody give to examine, Justices, the leader of that mighty expedition against Troy, or else Odysseus, or Sisyphus, or a myriad of others one might mention, men and women too? There to talk with them, consort with them, examine them, would be a happiness beyond compare! Surely there, I take it, they do not put a man to death for doing that; for, happy in all else, people are happier there than here in that henceforth they are immortal, at all events if what is said is true.

But, Justices, you also it behoves to have good hope with reference to death, and this one thing you must bear in mind as true, that, living or dead, to a good man there can come no evil, nor are his affairs a matter of indifference to the gods. Nor has my destiny now come about by chance; rather, it is clear to me that it was better for me now to die and to be released from my troubles. That is why the sign did not at any point deter me, and why I am not very bitter at those who voted to condemn me, or at my accusers. It is true they did not have this notion in condemning and accusing me; no, they thought to injure me, and therein they merit blame.

One thing, however, I do beg of them. When my sons grow up, then, Gentlemen, I ask you to punish them, you hurting them the same as I hurt you, if they seem to you to care for money, or aught else, more than they care for virtue. And if they pretend to be somewhat when they are nothing, do you upbraid them as I upbraided you, for not regarding as important what they ought to think so, and for thinking they have worth when they do not. If you do that, I shall have received just treatment from you, and 42 my sons as well.

And now the time has come for our departure, I to die, and you to live. Which of us goes to meet the better lot is hidden from all unless it be known to God.

Crito

Crito

Crito, like *Euthyphro,* is in itself so open, clear, and brief, that no extended preface or long explanatory note to it is here demanded. Plato's writing is in general clear; the exceptions to that statement are mostly found in the allegories or illustrative tales. In *Crito* their place is taken by the apparition of the Laws, personified, with their hypothetical argument against any effort of Socrates to escape from prison and evade the capital punishment which has by law been set for him. This episode makes no difficulty for the reader. Sometimes, again, with a longer dialogue the reader may be helped by an outline of the whole that also marks the successive steps of an argument. But *Crito* is short; as we have seen, it runs to 4,100 words or thereabout; its outline and successive steps are plain.

Something may well be said on the desirability of bringing new readers to the dialogue *Crito* at the present time. No doubt, like *Gorgias,* it would have a telling message for men in every age of history since Plato wrote. But as *Gorgias* has a special message for the nations in our troubled times, when it still can persuade us that, though we ought not to suffer wrong when the suffering can without harm be avoided, yet it is better to suffer wrong than to do it; as *Gorgias* now has that special message for men and unjust leaders, so *Crito* has in our time, and in America, a special message for the young. No other writing outside of the Christian tradition is so persuasive toward respect for the law. And in our time and nation we have seen too many standards, ethical, social, and religious, denied and discarded by the young. No civilized nation, so-called, has witnessed more, or more open, disrespect for custom and law. On the one hand, we hear that human nature does not change; on the other, that the ethical and social laws that governed human nature and its welfare in the past are all of them outmoded. Granted that human nature has not changed, except that Christianity has greatly changed our ideals for the better; still, so far as human nature has remained the same, good ethics for the individual, good laws for the group, simply mean good habits, habits that are good for human life. Good ethics are just that; they are the means to the end of good living. *Crito* promotes respect for them. Doubtless it has had its share in cultivating that higher respect for law, both written and unwritten, which is characteristic of Great Britain and her colonies, as Canada, Australia, and New Zealand, in comparison with the lawlessness of our United States.

The unwritten law in the heart of Plato and his Socrates it is that keeps Socrates in prison to die, when he might have escaped. At a venture we may suggest to the reader of the dialogue that he read also an article or address called *Law and Manners,* by Lord Moulton, which appeared in the *Atlantic Monthly* 134 (1924). 1–5. From this we make room to quote two short passages. First (p. 2):

This country which lies between Law and Free Choice I always think of as the domain of Manners. To me, Manners in this broad sense signifies the doing that which you should do although you are not obliged to do it.

And thus Lord Moulton closes (p. 5):

Now I can tell you why I chose the title 'Law and Manners.' It must be evident to you that Manners must include all things which a man should impose upon himself, from duty to good taste. I have borne in mind the great motto of William of Wykeham—*Manners makyth Man.* It is in this sense—loyalty to the rule of Obedience to the Unenforceable, throughout the whole realm of personal action—that we should use the word 'Manners' if we would truly say that 'Manners makyth Man.'

The Dialogues of Plato do not in spirit reach the level of our sacred Scriptures. Plato's monotheism is not the clear concept which we find in the Mosaic Law. And yet when we have read the *Apology* and *Crito* we do not find it hard to pass to the commandment recorded by Moses: 'Thou shalt have no other gods before me'; or to the summary of Christ:

Thou shalt love the Lord thy God with all thy heart, and with all thy soul, and with all thy mind. This is the first and great commandment. And the second is like unto it: Thou shalt love thy neighbor as thyself. On these two commandments hang all the law and the prophets.[1]

[1] Matt. 22.37–40.

Crito

SOCRATES and CRITO [in Dialogue. Crito visits Socrates in Prison.]

SOCRATES. What brings you here at this time, Crito? Or is n't it still 43 early?

CRITO. Indeed it is.

SOCRATES. How early?

CRITO. The earliest dawn.

SOCRATES. I marvel that the keeper of the prison was willing to let you in.

CRITO. He has got used to me now, Socrates, because I am so often here, and besides he has had a tip from me.

SOCRATES. Did you come just now or some time since?

CRITO. Quite a little while ago.

SOCRATES. Well then, why did n't you wake me up right off? Why did you sit there by me, and not say a word?

CRITO. By Heaven, Socrates, if I were in your place I should n't wish to be awake so long and grieving; no, and I have all this while been wondering to see how peacefully you sleep. And I purposely did not wake you, for I wanted you to pass the time most pleasantly. Indeed, throughout your life ere now, I have often thought you fortunate in your disposition, but never so much as in this present pass when I see how easily and quietly you take it.

SOCRATES. But really, Crito, at my age it would be out of place to take it ill because I had to die.

CRITO. Yes, Socrates, but other men of a comparable age are caught in toils like these, but their age does not release them from distress at their present lot.

SOCRATES. That is true. But why now have you come so early?

CRITO. Socrates, I bring a piece of news that is grievous and heavy, as it seems to me, not to you but to me and all your nearest friends;

so grievous and heavy, I say, that I cannot think of anything so hard for me to bear.

SOCRATES. What news? You mean that the ship has come back from Delos, on whose arrival I must die?

CRITO. She has not yet arrived; but I take it she will arrive to-day; so I judge from what some people report who have come from Sunium and left her there. From their report it is clear that she will come to-day, and so to-morrow, Socrates, your life will have to end.

SOCRATES. Well, Crito, that is no bad luck. If that is the will of the gods, let it be so. All the same, I think she will not come to-day.

44 CRITO. What makes you think so?

SOCRATES. I will tell you. The fact is, I must die on the next day after the ship comes in.

CRITO. That is what they say who have the matter in charge.

SOCRATES. Well then, I think that she will not come to-day, but will arrive to-morrow. My ground for thinking so is a dream I had a little earlier in the night. And so it was a timely thing that you did not wake me.

CRITO. What sort of dream did you have?

SOCRATES. I thought I saw a woman coming to me, beautiful and stately, clad in white, who called to me, and said: 'Socrates,

The third day you shall reach the fertile plain of Phthia.'

CRITO. A singular dream that, Socrates.

SOCRATES. Full of meaning, Crito, as it seems to me.

CRITO. Far too full, I take it. But, my dearest Socrates, do finally listen to me now, and save yourself. For my part, if you die, it will not be just one misfortune; not merely shall I be deprived of such a friendship as I never again shall find the like of; but, more than that, to many who do not know you and me too well, I shall seem like one who could have saved you had he been willing to spend the money, and did not care to do it. Now, tell me, is there any reputation worse than that of seeming to put money above friends? The crowd will never believe that it was you yourself who would not get out of here, while we were eager for it.

SOCRATES. But, my blessed Crito, why should we care so much for the opinion of the crowd? It is the best men, rather, who deserve consideration, they who think that a thing occurs precisely as it does.

CRITO. But, Socrates, you surely see that we have to reckon with the opinion of the crowd as well. The present situation makes it clear that the crowd can work, not very little evils, but well-nigh the greatest, when any one is slandered among them.

SOCRATES. Would that the crowd did, Crito, have the power to work the greatest of evils, for then they could also work the greatest good, and all would be well. As things are, they can do neither. They cannot make anybody either wise or foolish, and they do whatever they do by chance.

CRITO. Have it as you wish. But tell me, Socrates. Isn't the thing that holds you back your fear for me and the rest of your friends? You fear that, if you left this place, the sycophants would make trouble for us on the charge that we had stolen you away, and we should be forced to give up all our fortune, or a tremendous sum of money, and pay some other penalty besides? If you fear any- 45 thing like that, be of an easy mind. In order to rescue you, it is right for us to run this risk, and, if need be, greater. No, listen to me, and don't do otherwise.

SOCRATES. That does prevent me, Crito, but there are other things besides.

CRITO. Well, have no fear about the matter. The sum of money is, in fact, not large which certain persons are ready to accept in order to save you and get you out of here. Then, for the informers don't you see how cheaply one can buy them off, and it doesn't take much money to deal with them? My own fortune is at your service, and I believe it is enough. Further, if you care for me, and think you ought not to spend my money, there are our friends from elsewhere who are ready to spend theirs. One of them, Simmias of Thebes, has actually brought the right amount for this very end. Cebes is ready too, and a great many others. So, as I say, do not hesitate to save yourself for fear of that, nor make a difficulty of the thing you spoke of in court, that you would not know what to do with yourself in exile. Abroad they would cherish you everywhere on your arrival. If you wish to go to Thessaly, there I have friends who will make much of you, and give you a safe retreat so that nobody there can annoy you.

Further, Socrates, I think you are not doing what is right in aiming to betray yourself when your safety rests with you. You are bent on having the sort of thing happen to you that your enemies and those who wish to ruin you are eager, and were eager, to see happen. In addition to that, it seems to me you are betraying your own sons as well; when it rests with you to rear and educate them, you desert them, and for your part they may fare as chance will have it; and their lot is likely to be the usual destitute lot of orphans. Either we ought never to beget them, or, having children, we must carry out the task of rearing them and seeing to their education; but you appear to me to pick the easiest way. It is our duty, though, to choose the way of the true, courageous man, and take it, above all if one has professed to be concerned about virtue all one's life.

As for me, I am ashamed, both for you and for all of us your friends, for fear the whole affair concerning you may seem to have been handled with a certain lack of vigor on our part, from the beginning of the case and your appearance at court when you need not have appeared, and the actual conduct of the trial with its outcome, to this final, as it were ridiculous, close of the whole action. It will look as if through cowardice and a lack of vigor on our part we had let things get away from us when we failed to save you and you failed to save yourself, when it was feasible and possible if we had been a bit of use. Consider all this, Socrates; do n't let the harm be joined with shame for you and us. No, decide, or rather it is no longer the time to decide; the decision should have been made. There is but one. Everything must be done this coming night. If we delay, the thing cannot be done, will be no longer feasible. No, Socrates, by all means listen to me, and do just what I say.

SOCRATES. Dear Crito, your helpfulness is of great value, if it squares with what is right. If not, the more you try to help, the harder you make it. We have to study whether we should do all this, or not; as for me, not only now, but always, it has been my rule to follow no other of my leanings save the reason that, upon consideration, appeared to me to be the best. The arguments which I have uttered hitherto, I cannot now reject when this thing by chance has come upon me; no, they appear to me to be substantially the same as ever, and I respect and honor the same ones as before. And so, if we have none better than these to offer in the present case, you may rest assured that I will not give in to you; no, not if the power of the crowd essayed to scare us like children with more bogies than at present, by letting loose against us chains and executions and robberies of our wealth. Well then, how are we to make the test as fairly as we can? We may do it if we first take up this notion which you uttered on the subject of opinions, and see whether it was right or not to say that one must always pay attention to some views, and not to others. Or was that statement valid before I had to die, and is there evidence now that it was only made for the sake of argument, and in fact was only fun and nonsense? I wish to study the assertion, Crito, together with you, to see if it is going to look different, now that my case stands thus, or just the same, and whether we are going to dismiss or follow it. The statement always made, I think, by persons who speak seriously, and what I myself just now asserted, is approximately this. Of the opinions which men entertain there are some that we must take as of great value, and some that we must not. Before Heaven, Crito! does n't this statement strike you as sound? As far as human foresight goes, you are not called upon to die to-morrow, and the present juncture will not distort your judgment. 47 Does n't it strike you as a valid statement that not all the opinions entertained by men are to be regarded, but some should be, and some should not, nor the opinions of all men, but those of some should be accepted, those of others not? What do you say? Is n't that a valid statement?

CRITO. It is valid.

SOCRATES. And the good opinions are to be regarded, the bad ones not?

CRITO. Yes.

SOCRATES. And the good opinions come from men of sense, the bad come from the senseless?

CRITO. That is certain.

SOCRATES. Come now. Let us see what we meant by talking thus. Take a man who is in training, and gives himself to that. Does he pay attention to everybody's praise, blame, and opinion, or only to the views of that one man who happens to be a doctor or gymnastic trainer?

CRITO. To the views of one man only.

SOCRATES. And so the criticism one must fear, the praise one is to welcome, are those of that one man; they are not those of the crowd.

CRITO. That is clear.

SOCRATES. Thus the man must act and exercise and eat and drink in the way that seems correct to the one individual who is his master, and who understands him, rather than to all the others put together.

CRITO. That is right.

SOCRATES. So be it. But suppose he disobeys the one, and disregards his praises and opinion, respecting instead the arguments of the crowd who have no understanding; will he not meet with some evil?

CRITO. He surely will.

SOCRATES. What sort of evil, whither tending, and affecting what in him who disobeys?

CRITO. Manifestly, it will tend to harm his body; this it will destroy.

SOCRATES. Well said. And as to other matters, Crito, we can say the same, without our having to go through them all. And so it is with respect to right and wrong, the ugly and the beautiful, and the good and bad, which are the subject of our present consultation; the question being whether we should follow the opinion of the crowd, and be afraid of that, or the opinion of the one, if there is a man of understanding whom we ought to reverence, and to fear, more than all the others put together; a person such that, if we do not follow him, we shall injure and destroy that which, we said, improves through justice, and is ruined by injustice. Or does that mean nothing?

CRITO. I think as you do, Socrates.

SOCRATES. Well then, take that which is made better by the wholesome [by a healthful régime], and is ruined by unwholesome measures when we injure it by following the judgment of those who do not understand; when we do so, is our life worth living? And the thing in question is the body, is it not?

CRITO. Yes.

SOCRATES. Well, is life worth living with a bad and ruined body?

CRITO. It is not.

SOCRATES. Then is life worth living when that part of us is ruined to which wrong does harm, and right does good? Or do we think the body is more worthy than that part of us, whatever it may be, 48 with which injustice and righteousness are concerned?

CRITO. We do not.

SOCRATES. Is not this more worthy?

CRITO. More by far.

SOCRATES. So, best of friends, in no case do we need to pay attention to what the crowd will say of us; we need only consider what he will say who understands about things right and wrong, he and Truth itself. Accordingly, here first of all you did not follow the right path, in taking the position that we ought to heed the notions of the crowd concerning justice, beauty, and goodness and their opposites. Meanwhile, of course, some one might say that the crowd has power to kill us.

CRITO. All that is certain, Socrates, and some one might affirm it.

SOCRATES. You are right. But, my good friend, this argument we have followed through still strikes me in the same way as before. And look at the other again; see if it does or does not hold for us that what most counts is not to live, but is to live aright.

CRITO. Yes, that still holds.

SOCRATES. And the argument still holds that living well and beautifully and justly are all one thing? Does that still hold, or not?

CRITO. It holds.

SOCRATES. Then it is from these positions that we must proceed to inquire whether it is right for me to go out from here without leave from the Athenians, or is wrong. And if we see that it is right, we shall try to do it; if not, we shall give it up. For the other considerations you bring up, questions of expense, of reputation, of the children's education, be careful, Crito; they may well be the concerns of that great crowd who, lacking all intelligence, lightly put to death, and would as lightly bring to life again, if they were able. For us, since reason will have it so, there is no other question to be solved than what we just now said, whether we shall be doing right in giving money, and thanks as well, to those who will get me out of here, and you in leading and I in being led away, or whether we shall in truth be wrong in doing all these things. And if we shall clearly be doing wrong if we proceed to do them, there is no alternative but to reckon whether we ought not to stay here quietly and die, or to suffer anything else whatever, rather than do wrong.

CRITO. I think that what you say is valid, Socrates. See what we have to do.

SOCRATES. Let us look at it together, my friend, and if you have any argument to urge against me, argue, and I will yield to you. Otherwise, dear fellow, stop telling the same story over, and saying I must get away from here against the will of the Athenians; I prize your efforts to persuade me to it, but shall not do it from compulsion. Observe the basis, now, of the inquiry, to see if it is adequately put for you, and try to answer what is asked according to your best capacity.

CRITO. Indeed I will.

SOCRATES. We ought never, shall we say, willingly to do wrong? Or are there circumstances under which wrong may be done, while under others it may not? Or is wrongdoing never good, and never beautiful, as we often have agreed heretofore? It is what we have just stated now. Or are all the positions we have hitherto agreed on to be given up within these last few days? At our age, Crito, is it possible that we old men have been seriously conversing all this time, without perceiving that our talk was on a level with the talk of boys? Is it not far rather true that the matter stands precisely as was stated by us then, whether it is what the crowd asserts or not? And whether we must endure a lot still worse than this, or a better, under any circumstances doing w g is bad and shameful for the doer? Is that what we assert, or not?

CRITO. We assert it.

SOCRATES. In no case, then, should one do wrong.

CRITO. No indeed.

SOCRATES. Nor should anybody who is wronged retaliate with wrong, as most people think; because it is one's duty never to do wrong.

CRITO. Clearly not.

SOCRATES. Further, should one do anybody evil, Crito? Yes or no?

CRITO. Surely not, Socrates.

SOCRATES. Well then, what of doing evil in return for evil, as most people say you should? Is it right, or wrong?

CRITO. It is never right.

SOCRATES. No doubt because doing evil to a man is just the same as doing wrong.

CRITO. That is true.

SOCRATES. So one ought not to return injustice, nor do evil to anybody in the world, no matter what one may have suffered from them. And in making this admission, Crito, see that what you grant does not run counter to your own belief; for I know that few hold this opinion, or will hold it. And those who do and those who do not hold it have no common ground when they deliberate; no, they necessarily despise each other as soon as they see each other's decisions. Do you too, then, look well to see if you have common ground with me, and share my view, and we begin deliberations from this point, namely, that it never is correct to act unjustly, or repay a wrong with wrong, or, when one suffers evil, to defend oneself by doing evil in return; or do you withdraw from that position, and not share this principle with me? For my part, I have long since held to that, and do so now. As for you, if you have reached another view, say so, and explain it. But if you hold to what you held before, listen to what follows upon that.

CRITO. I do still hold to that, and do agree with you. You may go on.

SOCRATES. Then I go on to say what follows; or rather I will ask the question whether, after we agree with some one that a thing is right, we should do it, or should break our word?

CRITO. We should do it.

SOCRATES. From that point look carefully at this. If we go out of here without obtaining the permission of the City, shall we not be doing ill to certain persons, and precisely those whom we ought least of all to injure? And are we holding by what we agreed was right, or not?

CRITO. I am unable, Socrates, to answer, for I do not understand your question.

SOCRATES. Well, look at it in this way. Suppose that we were on the point of running away from here, or give it whatever name it ought to have, and suppose the Laws and the civic commonwealth were to come and confront us, and to ask: 'Tell us, Socrates, what have you in mind to do? With this deed you have in hand do you mean aught else than to destroy us, us the Laws, and all the State, so far as in you lies? Do you think it possible for a city to continue, not to be overturned, in which the decisions that are rendered have no force, but are made of no effect and done away with by private individuals?' What are we going to answer, Crito, to these questions, and to others like them? In defence of that law destroyed, a man, an orator above all, might utter many arguments; the law which decrees that judgments rendered shall be supreme! Are we going to say, 'But the State has done us wrong, and has not given us a righteous judgment'? Is that what we shall say?

CRITO. By Heaven, Socrates, just that!

SOCRATES. Well now, suppose the Laws should answer: 'Socrates, was that the agreement between us and you, or was it not that you should hold by such decisions as the City renders?' And if we were astonished when they spoke that way, they might well add: 'You need not wonder, Socrates, at what we say; no, answer us, since you are in the habit of employing question and reply. Come now, what have you to complain of in us, and in the City, that you should set about destroying us? First of all, did you not owe your birth to us, and through us did not your father take your mother and engender you? Say then, have you any quarrel with those of us Laws that have to do with marriage, on the ground of their imperfection?' 'No,' I would say, 'I have n't.' 'Well, what of those about the rearing of the offspring and their education, which you too received? Did we not order matters well, those of us who have these things in charge, when we gave directions to your father to have you trained in music and gymnastic?' 'Yes,' I would answer, 'you did well.' 'So be it. And after you were born, and reared, and educated, could you in the first place say you are not ours, our progeny, our bondman, yourself along with all your line? And if the case stands thus, do you think that you and we are on a level with respect to justice, so that what we undertake to do to you, you can justly do again to us? Suppose it were only your father, or your master—if you had one; would you be on a level with him in regard to justice, so that you could give him back the treatment 51 you received from him, answer evil word with evil, strike him back when he struck you, and all the rest? But now it is your fatherland, it is the Laws; and with respect to us is it allowed to you, if we are minded to destroy you because we think it right, is it for you to try, as far as you are able, to do away with us, the Laws, and your fatherland as well? And you will say that when you do so you are acting justly, you the man who verily cares so much for virtue! Are you so wise as to forget that more than mother, father, ancestors one and all, a man must honor his country; that the fatherland is more to be revered, more holy, takes a higher place in the opinion both of gods and men who have intelligence? Yes, one must reverence the fatherland, and yield and soften more to it when it is harsh than to one's father, and either win it to one's side or do what it commands, and suffer quietly what it enjoins, whether that means to be beaten, to be put in chains, or to be led to war and there be wounded or slain. One must do it all, for that is what justice demands. One must not weaken, nor flinch, nor leave one's post, but in war, in court, and everywhere one must do what the City and fatherland enjoins, or else win her over with means that are by nature right. If it is impious to use violence against a mother, or a father, how much worse is violence against the fatherland?' What shall we say to all that, Crito? Shall we answer that the Laws are wrong or right?

CRITO. I take it they are right.

SOCRATES. 'Look, then, Socrates,' the Laws might add; 'see if we are right in saying that you do injustice to us when you try to do what you are now attempting. We who bore you, reared you, taught you, let you share with all the other citizens in all the goods at our disposal, do nevertheless proclaim to every one of the Athenians who chooses, that, as soon as he has qualified as citizen, and knows how things are done at Athens, and us the Laws, he is at liberty, if he does not like us, to take his property and go wherever he desires. Not one of us stands in the way, or forbids it. Any one of you who wishes, if he does not like us and the City, may go off into a colony, or may go away and live elsewhere in foreign parts; he may go wherever he desires, taking his belongings with him.

'But if any of you stays, when he can see our way of dealing justice, and our way of managing the State in other things, we contend that by his act he has agreed with us to do what we enjoin; and we assert that he who will not yield does triple wrong, because he does not yield to us who gave him being, nor to us who reared him, and, having promised to obey us, he neither does so nor persuades us if in aught we have done ill. Meanwhile we make our proposals, and do not roughly bid him do what we command; no, we give him the alternative of persuading us or doing what we say; but he does neither. Now, Socrates, we say to you that you are going to be open to these charges if you do what you think of doing, and you, not open least, but, among the citizens of Athens, you above all others.'

Suppose I said: 'Why so?' Perhaps they would rightly upbraid me by saying that of the Athenians I was one who above all others had consented to the said agreement. They would tell me: 'Socrates, we have strong evidence that you were pleased with us and with the City. Far beyond the rest of the Athenians you steadily dwelt in her, and you never would have done so if she had not pleased you to a high degree, and you never went out of the City to a festival save to the Isthmus, once, and never visited an alien country save on military service, nor made any other journey as do other men, nor were seized with a desire to know another State and other laws; no, with us you were content, and with our City. So decidedly did you prefer us, and agreed to live our civic life in every way, and in particular begot your children in the City, a sign that you were pleased with her. Further, in the trial itself, it was allowed you, if you chose, to set the penalty at exile, and what you think of doing now against the will of the City, you could have done then with her leave. Then you made a show of not being grieved if you had to die; rather, so you stated, you chose death in preference to exile. To-day you feel no shame about those words, nor any reverence for us Laws whom you are minded to destroy; you are doing what the most good-for-nothing slave would do, attempting to run off in spite of compacts and agreements you have made with us to act the part of citizen. First of all, then, tell us this; say whether we are right in holding that you agreed to be a citizen with respect to us in deed, and not in word. Are we right, or are we not?' What, Crito, shall we say to that? Anything save that we admit it?

CRITO. We are forced to grant it, Socrates.

SOCRATES. 'What else are you doing, then,' they would go on, 'but running counter to your compacts with us, and agreements which you entered into under no compulsion and through no deceit? Nor were you forced to choose in haste; no, you had seventy years in which it was permitted you to go away if you did not like us, and if our agreements seemed to you to be unjust. But you did not prefer either Sparta or Crete, which you constantly bring forward as examples of good government, nor any other State, Hellenic or barbarian; no, you got away from Athens less than any lame or blind man or other crippled person. So obvious is it that you liked the City and us the Laws beyond anybody else of the Athenians; for who will like a city if he does not like its laws? Yet now you do n't abide by your agreements? You would if you believed us, Socrates, and would not become an object of derision through your exit from the City!

'Reflect, now. If you transgress and err in this, what good will you accomplish for yourself or for your friends?—for it is pretty clear that your friends themselves will run the risk of exile, deprivation of their civic rights, and loss of fortune. For yourself first of all, if you betake yourself to one of the cities that are nearest, to Thebes or Megara—for both have excellent laws—you will come as an enemy, Socrates, to their State, and all the people there who care about their city will view you with suspicion as a man who will destroy the laws, and you will confirm the reputation of your judges here, and make it seem as if the decision they gave was right; for doubtless any one who violates the laws is sure to be regarded as a person likely to corrupt the youth and foolish men. Must you, then, avoid well-governed cities and the most law-abiding men? And if you do so, will your life be worth the living? Or will you mingle in their life, and, unashamed, go on discussing with them—what subjects, Socrates? The same as here? Will you argue that righteousness and virtue are the things of most account to men, along with law and order? And don't you think that in so doing Socrates would cut a sorry figure? The thought is inescapable.

'But perhaps you will avoid these places, and go to Thessaly to visit with the friends of Crito, for there one finds the utmost lack of discipline and order, and perhaps you will be heard with delight as you tell how in comic wise you escaped from prison with some sort of cloak about you, or hooded in a goatskin, or in some other such disguise as runaways are in the habit of employing, and with an alteration of your figure. That you, an aged man, with probably but little time remaining if you live, are not ashamed so eagerly to cling to life that you will break the highest laws—do you think that nobody will say so? Perhaps not, if you disturb nobody. Otherwise, Socrates, you will hear many despicable things said of you. You will live cringing before all men, servile to all—and doing what? Aught else save banqueting in Thessaly, as if you had gone off to Thessaly on invitation to a feast? And then those arguments of ours on justice and the whole realm of virtue, what will become of them? But what about the children for whom you wish to live in order to rear and educate them? How now?

Will you take them into Thessaly, and rear and educate them there, and make them aliens, that so they may have this benefit to thank you for as well? Or no, not that, but rather that, while you are yet alive, they may get their rearing and education here, the better for your absence from them? Your friends would care for them. They would care for them if you departed into Thessaly, whereas if you departed into Hades they would not? But if those who profess to be your friends are good for anything, they would. One surely must believe it.

'No indeed, Socrates, listen to us who have reared you, and do not put your children, or your life, or anything else, above the right. Then when you arrive in Hades, you can offer all this in your defence to those who govern there; for, clearly, here on earth what you are doing is not the better thing for you, nor juster, nor more pious, nor is it so for any of your friends, nor will it be better for you after your arrival there. No; if you now depart this life, you go condemned unjustly, not by us the Laws, but by men. But if you escape, thus basely returning wrong for wrong, evil for evil, breaking your own agreement and your compact with us, and working ill for those who least of all should suffer it, yourself, your friends, the fatherland, and us, then here we shall be angry at you living, and there our brethren the Laws in Hades will not receive you gladly, knowing that, so far as it lay with you, you attempted to destroy us. No, do not let Crito move you to do what he advises; listen rather to us.'

That, you may rest assured, my dear friend Crito, that is what I take it I am hearing, as the Corybantic revelers think they hear the flutes; yes, the sound of these words is ringing in me, and keeps me from hearing all else. So be sure that so far as my positions now are taken, whatever you may say against them you will say in vain. And yet, if you imagine you can do aught further, speak.

CRITO. No, Socrates, I have nothing to say.

SOCRATES. So, Crito, let the matter rest, and let us act thus since it is the way in which God leads us.

Phaedo

Phaedo

The dialogue begins, as it were, after some words have passed between Echecrates and Phaedo, who has just arrived in Phlius, a few words, one might imagine of preliminary greeting. Plato does not wish you to think about them. He breaks into the middle of a conversation, yet opens with a true beginning which leads without delay to the proper subject.

Of Phlius little is known. The residence or gathering-place of some Pythagoreans, it was a small town to the South-east of Corinth and the Isthmus, ten miles or so to the North-west of ancient Mycenae. To the North-east, beyond the Isthmus lay Megara, a city of culture, and of interest to Plato, to which he retired after Socrates was dead, in order to be away from Athens, and to be with his friend the mathematician Euclid and others of the Socratic group. Megara is twenty miles West of Athens; as from it, Euclid (Eucleides) and Terpsion are mentioned among those who were with Socrates at Athens on the final day. Simmias and Cebes, also Pythagoreans, and, with Socrates, chief speakers in the dialogue as Phaedo reports it, were both of them pupils of Philolaus at Thebes. Phaedo, who tells Echecrates of Socrates' last day and conversation, is an Athenian youth young enough for Socrates to play with his hair, perhaps ten years younger than Plato, who would be twenty-eight years old [1] when Socrates died, and who doubtless then knew Phaedo well. They would still have been in touch when Phaedo was mature, some years later when the dialogue was written; there is, however, no hint that he was Plato's main source of information regarding the events of that closing day; the assumption that a hearer could in after-years repeat the speeches of an extended dialogue is the same that we meet in the *Symposium,* where Apollodorus, present also in *Phaedo,* tells the story of that previous occasion. Plato could learn details for the dialogue of *Phaedo* from Apollodorus, Euclid, Cebes, Antisthenes, Terpsion, and others, as well as from Phaedo.

On the last day in prison Plato was not there. 'I believe,' says Phaedo,

---

[1] Assuming that Plato was born in the year 428/7 B. C.

'that he was sick'; the words give a pathetic touch. The only other direct references to Plato in his dialogues we have seen in the *Apology*, where Socrates names him among those who are ready to advance the money for a fine. It may well be that the last day as it approached was too much for him to bear, and that he wishes those who read his work to infer the reason for his illness.

The mention of his absence also allowed him more of an artistic freedom; more freedom to elaborate the dialogue as a work of art, and less of a seeming personal responsibility for recording the minute details of every argument. Not that we need doubt the substantial truth of the dialogue to the essential event and argument as they occurred; the occasion was too grave, and too many witnesses, still alive when the work was published, would object to manifest discrepancies between the record and the facts. But we must never forget that Plato's truth is general, universal, of a higher sort than mere literal accuracy or truth to unimportant detail.

This dialogue of, say, 21,500 words, as Plato makes his young friend report it, is four times as long as *Euthyphro*, five times as long as *Crito*. Among the works of Plato it is of intermediate length. It is easily divided into beginning, middle, and end. The middle, too, the longest part, is easily subdivided. The beginning and end make a surrounding frame for the substantial argument (with an extended myth) about the immortality or more strictly divinity and hence indestructibility of the soul; to this argument the doctrine of eternal forms is subjoined, along with the cosmological myth of the true surface of the earth and the subterranean geography of Tartarus and its rivers.

The beginning and end of *Phaedo* have specially impressed themselves upon the memory of mankind. Among many telling passages of Plato, one might well-nigh single them out as the most vivid. Concerning them one need say little beyond the praise that is demanded by Plato's wonderful and sagacious art. One point, however, relating to Xanthippe, may here be discussed; another, on the burial of Socrates, is reserved for the close of this note.

The notion that the wife of Socrates was a shrew is not derived from Plato, and must not be read into Socrates' request in the opening scene 'that she be taken away; she returns for the close, and when the conversation of the men is over, Socrates spends time in an adjoining room with his wife and family, off-stage as it were, before reappearing to us in the final scene to drink the cup. If there is any element of truth in the tradition that Xanthippe was a scold because of Socrates' devotion to his quest, and of their resultant poverty, Plato does not mar his work by breathing of it here—nor elsewhere. Here as elsewhere his dialogue, his dialogues, may be seen as a drama of the school and a school of good manners.

The middle bulk of the dialogue is duly subdivided. The question of immortality once launched, we have as evidence of survival the doctrine of rebirth, supported by the argument that opposites arise from opposites (so death from life, and life again from death, in an endless revolution), and as further evidence the doctrine of reminiscence; both doctrines well known to many readers through Wordsworth's use of them in his *Ode, Intimations of Immortality,* where yet the Platonism is not too distinct or pure. The doctrine of reminiscence is based upon the Socratic theory of forms, with which we must here deal quite briefly. This theory is again found in Socrates' reply (100 ff.; see below, pp. 169–80) to Simmias and Cebes; it is elucidated in other dialogues also, as the *Republic;* and because the subject has been controversial among scholars, the inquiring reader had best begin the study of it in John Burnet's edition of *Phaedo.*

From the traditional doctrines of rebirth and reminiscence (which must be, not taken singly, but combined), we go on to the second proof of immortality, a more cogent one derived from the argument that a true reality (form, idea) is indestructible, and that the soul is a reality of this description.

Now comes an interlude in which Socrates gives opportunity for objections. The opportunity is seized by Simmias and Cebes. Simmias objects that soul and body are related as are harmony and the lyre, and that the harmony must perish with the instrument. Cebes argues that the soul like a weaver may and often does weave many garments or bodies in succession, but perishes before the last one is finally dissolved. He accepts the doctrine of pre-existence, but not of ultimate survival. These depressing Pythagorean arguments of Simmias stir Socrates to encourage all the disputants and hearers not to lose heart in the practice of discussion or the ultimate victory of sound argument. First he deals with Simmias' objection, and refutes the view that the soul is a harmony; then he proceeds to answer Cebes, beginning with the story of his own disillusion over the book of Anaxagoras, and its failure to hold steadily to the principle of *Nous* or Mind as the First Cause. Socrates explains the method he himself developed for the business of investigation. His reply to Cebes constitutes the third and final argument for immortality, reposes, as we saw, upon a doctrine of eternal forms, here rather described as indestructible realities, of which the soul is one. It is a divine reality, timeless, pre-existing and also enduring for ever.

This middle part of the dialogue includes many beautiful and interesting notions, to some of which we shall return, and closes with the Myth, which is the most interesting item of all.

For this item it may be said that here, as in some other myths of Plato, for example in the *Republic* the allegory of the Cave, his description offers difficulties, at least to the modern reader. In *Phaedo* his view of the physical world and of the regions, with their rivers, underneath, is not immediately clear to our imagination; it may have been more readily grasped by Greek readers in the time of Plato. The geometer himself, the author, doubtless had in his mind a picture precise enough, as he thought, for the students he knew. For us one difficulty is removed when we see that the world, something more than the earth, includes the enveloping atmosphere and an upper surface; the whole which Plato has in mind embraces this envelope; on this outer surface is the terrestrial paradise, the lovely abode of the blest. And the world is at the centre of the universe. Readers will understand that before Plato, from the time of Plato down, and throughout the Middle Ages, the spherical shape of the earth was known to educated men.

For the rivers, the configuration of the underworld, and the gulf or chasm of Tartarus, piercing, not like Dante's cone of the Inferno to the centre, but through the centre, the student will do well to consult the work of an expert scholar such as Burnet in his edition of *Phaedo* as already mentioned. Some main points to remember are these. There are sections of Tartarus on either side of the centre of the earth, and toward this centre water tends to fall. A given stream will fall into the chasm, then, at a point that is nearer to the centre than the point from which it issued. A stream may issue out of Tartarus in one hemisphere, and fall into it at a lower point in the other. Or streams may issue in one hemisphere, and circling round the other, return to fall again into the chasm at a lower point in the same hemisphere. By 'lower' we mean always, nearer to the centre; for up and down are less exact, more popular, conceptions.

Now we may mention, with some excusable repeating, a number of more interesting and striking concepts in the dialogue. The Myth, for example, is in sharp contrast with the argument in the *Apology* that Socrates had no interest in things above or beneath the surface of the earth. There he refutes the charge that he concerned himself with matters of that sort; here, in *Phaedo,* he is teaching them, not as things to be certainly known, but of tenable belief. The Myth has scientific probability, so to speak, not certainty. The eternal verities in the argument preceding the Myth are scientific, certain. From them the indestructibility, divinity, or, as we say, immortality of the soul is deduced.

Let us add that the Myth does not run counter to Socrates' main interest, which is human nature. He brings in the world above and beneath with relation to mankind. As contrasted with the philosophies before him, which were occupied with the physics and stuff of the cosmos, the philosophy of Socrates concerns itself with human conduct. His doctrine is: I am a man; no real interest of men is alien to me. Like Dante, he sees the universe, under God, in relation to the doings and sufferings of men as they obey or disobey the law divine, and gain the fit reward of further action, good or bad. To repeat, then, his terrestrial myth in its physical aspect is subordinate to ethics.

Of the doctrine of reminiscence, and the transmigration of the soul, both Pythagorean doctrines, we have spoken. So also, in the general Introduction, of the catalytic emotional effect of smiles and tears conjoint at which Plato aims throughout the dialogue. We have also previously noticed the beautiful concept that philosophy is the practice of music, or as later writers would have it, deriving their notion from Plato, that human life as a whole should be ordered as a work of art. So Milton argues that if a man is to be a poet, the life from which the poetry shall issue must be itself a poem. With this noble concept we may join the one, not always seen exactly as it is presented in this dialogue, that the life of the philosopher is, not death or dying, but a 'rehearsal' of the state of being dead; in other words, the joyful practice, in advance, of the immortality of the soul, the state in which she is freed from the care and burden of the body. The body is a dungeon or a prison-house; as Wordsworth and many another have accepted the notion, in the main from the dialogue of Plato. Thus Philosophy, as far as may be in this life, is a release from the bodily dungeon, a rehearsal of death, to the end of pure untrammeled contemplation.

For the geographer, one very interesting concept is that of the terrestrial basins, of which Plato at first hand knows only that of the Mediterranean and the lands adjacent to it. Socrates assumes that there are many others, likewise dwelling-places of mankind. By extension, the Atlantic Ocean, surrounded by the lands of modern Europe and America, is seen to be a comparable basin or configuration. It is the sort of concept for the subject of Anthropogeography in which the great geographer Ratzel took delight.

The correct habit of observation in Plato and his Socrates is also seen in the remarks about the songs of birds and vital cries of other creatures (*Phaedo* 85; see below, p. 149). The song of the nightingale, the chanting of the cranes, must not be taken, as poetical tradition would have it, for laments. Their songs are songs of joy. And so the innovator Wordsworth is not quite so original as some have thought him when he deliberately changes the 'boding note' of the owl to 'joyous note'; or when, with Coleridge, he departs from Milton to make the singing of the nightingale, also, joyful; or when they depart from the most of mankind in taking the bray of an ass, not for a lugubrious cry but for a cry of vital joy, his song. So far as records go, the Platonic Socrates it was, not Wordsworth, who first insisted upon this rectified opinion. Thus here again we come upon a further debt, it may be, of Wordsworth to the Dialogues of Plato.

The concept of catharsis or purgation is certainly a most important one among the formative notions in *Phaedo*. But here we only mention it. Purification is a theme that runs through early myth and ritual, through epic poetry and tragic drama, through medicine and philosophy. If Aristotle was as much impressed by *Phaedo* as scholars hold, there must be some relation between catharsis in this dialogue and the purge of the emotions which we find discussed in the *Poetics;* though doubtless the emotional catharsis there referred to may have been a commonplace of literary criticism in his time. For Plato catharsis is the cleansing process of study, scholarship, philosophy. True study cleans the soul of dross. And thus the death of the philosopher, when the soul is freed from the body, must be for him a catharsis. 'We owe a cock to Aesculapius, Crito,' said Socrates at the last. Pedants have tried to find the reason outside of the dialogue. The last words of Socrates imply that now his soul is about to be utterly cleansed of the body, and for that he owes a debt to the god of healing.

The generation of opposites from opposites, a concept which we find in other dialogues, we have also marked among those that are notable in *Phaedo,* and, particularly, the concept of life arising from death. As Paul has it (1 Cor. 15.36): 'That which thou sowest is not quickened, except it die.' And so we come at length to the Platonic concept of immortality. Plato does not mean absorption of the soul at death into any sea of Being. He means a survival of the individual man, of Socrates, of Plato, of you and me, the indestructibility of the man in his essential spirit as we know him, with all his own knowledge and attainments and capacity for further learning, his knowledge of men and poetry, with a memory of his friends and his beloved. Matter-of-fact men in their usual mood, of course, have a hard time of it with this belief. A crowd of Greeks in Paul's day simply derided it. Plato here ascribes it to his Socrates, and does not make himself responsible for it. Aristotle does not teach it in his extant works, which are 'scientific'; it belongs rather to the realm of poetry, and would more naturally find a place in one of Aristotle's dialogues, which survive only in fragments. We are not to forget that his favorite among the works of Plato was *Phaedo.* Yet even the matter-of fact share in the mood of contemplation to which all are subject. All men have it, some have it more than most. And in that mood, when they look inward, they discover this belief abiding.

As for the noblest of our kind, immortality is a thing the poets and men of deepest insight have, almost to a man, always believed in. For the belief in immortality among the Greeks one should, of course, consult the work of Erwin Rohde entitled *Psyche,* though as Burnet says: [2] 'The best book on Greek beliefs about the soul has no chapter on Socrates.' Before Socrates, the Homeric notions about immortality, while distinct enough, are not too cheerful; our earthly life is much to be preferred to that which follows it. The Pythagoreans clearly had a better doctrine on the subject, to which, along with the Orphic doctrine, Socrates and Plato no doubt owed more than the arguments against Simmias and Cebes in *Phaedo* might seem to suggest. In the Eleusinian mysteries, again, a very important matter must surely have been the inculcation of a belief in personal immortality; such a play as the *Frogs* of Aristophanes reveals an influence of the mysteries upon common belief, a belief in survival which the comedy assumes, and does not make fun of.

It is, however, Plato to whom subsequent ages have been indebted for the most influential reasoned and articulate argument for the immortality of the soul, namely in this dialogue of *Phaedo.* If Paul transcends the argument, he nevertheless is heavily in debt to it. The influence of this argument has been, of course, direct and indirect; indirect, for instance, through Paul and Cicero, Augustine and Ambrose, the Neoplatonists, Italian writers like Ficino, the Cambridge Platonists, and Spenser, Milton, and Wordsworth. But the direct influence has, save

[2] *Plato's Phaedo,* Introduction, p. xlviii.

for the Middle Ages,[3] always broken in upon the indirect, so that they unite in one stream, along with the more potent influence of the Bible. For example, we may take a passage I have used elsewhere.[4] As Sir Philip Sidney's life was ending in the presence of Christian divines,

> Instantly after prayer, he entreated this quire of divine philosophers about him to deliver the opinion of the ancient Heathen touching the immortality of the soul; first to see what true knowledge she retains of her own essence, out of the light of herself; then to parallel with it the most pregnant authorities of the Old and New Testament.[5]

In spreading a belief in immortality the influence of the Bible has been more significant than the influence of Plato, to some extent because the Bible does not depend upon reasoned argument, though Paul reasons and argues on the subject. Still with him the belief is, as it must be, largely a matter of faith supported by witness, of the higher, the poetic, the religious imagination.

Of the Old Testament it is often said that the doctrine of immortality is not there characteristic. The statement that a belief in it is not found there is simply false: 'I am . . . the God of Abraham, the God of Isaac, and the God of Jacob.' Or take the twenty-third Psalm: 'I will dwell in the house of the Lord for ever.' Or study the book of Malachi, the neglected link between the Old Testament and the New, for the doctrine of the fatherhood of God and the brotherhood of man, in which the doctrine of immortality is implicit. The stories of Enoch, Samuel, and Elijah also involve it.

In the New Testament the belief is everywhere assumed: 'If it were not so, I would have told you.' Throughout, the doctrine of the fatherhood of God and the brotherhood of man necessarily involves the doctrine of survival; the notion of human pre-existence, save for the Son, the Elder Brother, is not found. For the rest, a Power which can create, sustain, and control our life in the present time can recreate or continue it hereafter. A loving Power, almighty, which gives us a taste of the eternal life on earth will continue our life in future. Our life here is a part of that eternal life. No part of the eternal life can be taken from it; no part can be subtracted from the whole.

[3] When, of the works of Plato, the *Timaeus* was better known than the rest.

[4] In my volume of translations, mentioned above, published by the Oxford University Press, pp. liv–lv.

[5] Fulke Greville, *Life of Sidney*, ed. by Nowell Smith, 1907, pp. 136–7.

The method by which Socrates was put to death deserves remark. The drug he swallowed is commonly called hemlock, and was known to the Greeks as *cōnion* (Latin *conium*); the effects of drinking it in a lethal dose seem to be those which are described in *Phaedo*. The effect of Socrates' death upon Athens and succeeding ages is rightly anticipated in the *Apology;* no doubt it was observed by Plato before he wrote. Socrates did not refuse to drink of the cup; the result of his martyrdom includes many dialogues of Plato with their incalculable influence in antiquity and ever after. His death has done more for humanity than his life could have done without it or the manner of it.

For the fact, and for the Athenian method of putting Socrates to death, there is this to be said, that, as usual, the many-headed multitude did not know what it was doing. But granted that the majority of his judges thought him worthy of death, or that in accordance with a recent view of our day, and the view to be found in the seventh Platonic Epistle, he was put to death for political reasons, on a trumped-up charge; at all events the way of his punishment was humane in comparison with the ways of capital punishment in other times and nations. Death from drinking hemlock-juice is more humane than crucifixion, beheading, or burning at the stake.

In the works of Plato no hint is given of the real answer to the question raised by Crito about the disposal of Socrates' body. We know nothing of the burial. His mortal remains would naturally be laid in the place where those of his people before him were buried, and to which Xanthippe's body and the bodies of his children would in time be taken. Otherwise we might imagine that the bones of Socrates might later have been removed, and placed in the grounds of the Academy where the body of Plato afterwards was buried. Disinterment for reburial was not unknown at Athens. Aristotle in his will evidently intends that the bones of his wife Pythias shall be taken up, for he directs that, according to her wish, they shall be buried with him.[6] Plato doubtless left the question about the funeral of Socrates unanswered in detail for a good artistic reason. We do not know where the body of Moses was laid, and all the more we think of Moses as undying.

[6] Diogenes Laertius 5.16; I owe this reference to Professor Glenn R. Morrow.

Phaedo

[Persons of the Dialogue]

ECHECRATES, PHAEDO, [APOLLODORUS, SOCRATES, CEBES, SIMMIAS, CRITO; Attendant of the Eleven].

ECHECRATES. . . . Phaedo, were you yourself with Socrates on the 57 day when he drank the poison in prison, or did you hear about it from another?

PHAEDO. I was with him there myself, Echecrates.

ECHECRATES. What did the man have to say before his death, and how was the end? I would gladly hear about it; for nobody goes any more from Phlius to visit Athens, nor has any one come in a long, long time from there as a visitor here who could give us a clear account of it all, beyond the fact that he drank the poison and died. For the rest, there was never a word.

PHAEDO. Did n't you even hear of the trial, and the way it went? 58

ECHECRATES. Yes, somebody brought us the news of that, and we were amazed that, whereas the trial occurred so long before, he appeared to have died much later. What was the meaning of that, Phaedo?

PHAEDO. For him, Echecrates, there was a chance concurrence of events. The day before the trial it happened that the poop was crowned with laurel of the ship which the Athenians send to Delos.

ECHECRATES. Well, and what is that?

PHAEDO. It is the ship, according to Athenian tradition, in which upon a time Theseus took the seven pairs [young men and maidens] to Crete. He saved their lives, and saved his own as well. As the story goes, the City had vowed to Apollo that, if they were saved, a pilgrimage should be duly made each year to Delos. It is the mission which, from that day to the present, they annually send in honor of the god. Accordingly, the moment they begin the rite, throughout the period of the mission, it is their law that the City be kept free from stain, and no civic execution shall occur till the ship has gone to Delos and returned again to port. On occasion this requires no little time, if they happen to be caught by unfavorable winds. The beginning of the rite comes when the poop of the ship is crowned by the priest of Apollo. This happened, as I said, on the day before the judgment was pronounced; and that is why the time in prison was so long for Socrates between his condemnation and his death.

ECHECRATES. But what about the circumstances of his death itself? What was said and done, and who among his friends were with him? Or would the magistrates allow nobody to be present? Did he have to die, instead, bereft of friends?

PHAEDO. Not at all. There were several persons with him; yes, a goodly number.

ECHECRATES. Now you must tell us all about it, please, just as faithfully as you can, unless you do not happen to have any leisure.

PHAEDO. But indeed I am at leisure, and will try to tell you the whole story. For my part, I always take the utmost satisfaction in recalling Socrates, whether I myself am talking or listening to another.

ECHECRATES. Yes, Phaedo, and the same holds true of those who listen to you. Come now, try to tell us as precisely as you can everything that happened.

PHAEDO. For myself, the feelings I experienced there beside him were amazing. Within I felt no pity such as I might feel when present at the death of a dear friend, for to me, Echecrates, he seemed to be a happy man, alike in his bearing and his words, so fearlessly and nobly did he meet his end; so that he struck me, even on his way to Hades, as one who went, not without divine allotment, but, if ever man did, to fare well on his arrival there. That is why I felt no pity whatsoever, though pity would seem natural in a grievous situation; nor yet did I experience the pleasure we were wont to have together in philosophy, though of such sort our discussion actually was. No, the emotion I experienced was simply indescribable, a novel blend made up of pleasure, and pain therewith at the thought that he was just about to die. And all of us there present were in much the same condition, sometimes laughing, often weeping, and one of us, Apollodorus, going to extremes. You doubtless know the man, and his behavior.

ECHECRATES. I do indeed.

PHAEDO. Well, such was his experience above all; but I myself was deeply moved, and similarly the rest.

ECHECRATES. But who were present, Phaedo?

PHAEDO. Among local citizens, in addition to the said Apollodorus, Critobulus was present, and his father [Crito]; also Hermogenes, Epigenes, Aeschines, and Antisthenes; Ctesippus of Paeania, too, was there, and Menexenus and some other local persons. Plato, I believe, was sick.

ECHECRATES. There were some from other places?

PHAEDO. Yes, Simmias, Cebes, and Phaedondes, from Thebes; and from Megara Eucleides and Terpsion.

ECHECRATES. What of Aristippus and Cleombrotus? Were they present?

PHAEDO. They were not; it was said that they were in Aegina.

ECHECRATES. Was there anybody else?

PHAEDO. I believe I have mentioned virtually everybody there.

ECHECRATES. Well, go on. What did they discuss?

PHAEDO. I will try to tell you everything from the beginning. In the days preceding we had been accustomed, all of us, to visit Socrates each day; we met at dawn in the court where the trial had taken place, since it was near the prison. There we waited every morning, passing the time in conversation till the prison should be opened, for it did not open very early. When the door was opened, we went in to Socrates, and mostly spent the day with him. But on that day we met earlier; for the day before, as we left the prison at dusk, we learned that the ship had arrived from Delos. So we agreed with one another to come as early as we could to the usual place. So we did, and the keeper who was wont to let us in came out to us and told us we must wait, and not approach until he bade us do so; 'for,' said he, 'the Eleven are having Socrates unshackled, thereby informing him that he must die to-day.' After no long delay he came and bade us enter.

60   So we went in, and found Socrates just unshackled, and Xanthippe (his wife, you know) holding their little boy and sitting beside her husband. As soon as she saw us, Xanthippe greeted us with a cry, uttering the sort of thing that women are wont to do: 'O Socrates, this is the last time your friends will ever talk with you, or you with them!' And Socrates, turning to Crito, said: 'Crito, let some one take her home.' And some of Crito's people led her away shrieking and beating her breast.

Socrates, however, sat down upon his couch, drew up his leg, and rubbed it with his hand, and, as he rubbed it, said: 'What a singular thing it is, my friends, this thing which men call "pleasant"! How strangely allied it is by nature to what passes for its opposite, the painful! The two will not exist together in man, and yet if you pursue the one, and take it, you are virtually always forced to take the other also, as if, while two, they yet were fastened to a single head. It seems to me,' said he, 'that if Aesop had thought of this, he might have made a fable of it, thus: The Deity, wishing to compose their strife, and not succeeding, fastened their heads together into one; and that is why when one of them is present with a man, the other follows on behind. That is the way it seems to go with me; first there was the pain in my leg from the fetter, and here the pleasure appears coming after.'

[CEBES.]   Then Cebes rejoined: 'By Heaven, Socrates,' he said, 'I thank you for reminding me. About your poems, the tales of Aesop you have set to music, and the Prelude to Apollo; various persons have asked me about them, and in particular, two days ago, Evenus wished to know how it was that since you came hither you were minded to write poetry, whereas before you never did so. If it makes any difference to you whether I can satisfy Evenus when he asks me again—for I am sure he will do it—tell me what to say.'

[SOCRATES.]   'Why, Cebes,' he replied, 'just tell him the truth. Say that in composing them I had no wish to rival him or his poems, either; to do that, I knew, would not be easy. No, it was my aim to test the meaning of certain dreams, and to satisfy my conscience, if this was the music they repeatedly ordered me to make. The dreams were much like this. In the course of my life the same dream often has come to me, sometimes appearing in a different guise, but always saying the self-same thing: "Socrates," it would say, "make and practise music." And heretofore I took what I actually did to be the very thing I was urged to do and encouraged in doing; as people encourage the runners, so I thought the dream encouraged 61 me to go on in what I was doing, practising music, because philosophy was the highest kind of music, and this was what I was doing. But ever since the trial occurred and the feast of the god put off my death, I thought that if the dream perchance enjoined on me to make this music in the popular sense, I ought not to disobey it, but should make the music. It would be safer not to depart before I satisfied my conscience by composing poetry in obedience to the dream. So first I composed a piece to the god of the current sacrificial rite. After honoring the god, so I thought, the poet, if he really was to be a poet, ought next to make imaginative stories [MYTHS], not real narratives [LOGOI], but I was no mythographer, and so such myths as I had ready at hand, for I knew the fables of Aesop by heart, I took, and these I wrought as the first I hit upon. So tell that to Evenus, Cebes, salute him, and counsel him, if he is wise, to come right after me as quickly as he can. As for me, I leave, it appears, to-day, for so the Athenians command.'

[SIMMIAS.]   Then Simmias said: 'A wonderful exhortation, Socrates, to give Evenus! I have often met the man, and from what I have seen of him, it is pretty clear that he will not be willing in the least to listen to your counsel.'

[SOCRATES.]   'What!' said he. 'Is not Evenus a philosopher?'

[SIMMIAS.]   'I take him for one,' said Simmias.

[SOCRATES.]   'In that case, he, like everybody else who shares in this concern [philosophy], will listen, though doubtless he will do no violence to himself, since that, they say, is not permitted.' So saying, he let his legs down to the ground, and in this posture continued the discussion.

[CEBES.]   Then Cebes asked him: 'What is your meaning, Socrates, when you say it is not permitted to do violence to oneself, while yet the philosopher should wish to follow him who dies?'

[SOCRATES.]   'What, Cebes! Have you never heard the like of that, Simmias and you, when both of you were in the company of Philolaus?'

[CEBES.]   'Nothing certain, Socrates.'

[SOCRATES.]   'Well, all I know about it comes from hearsay, and surely there can be no objection to my telling what I happen to have heard. Meanwhile it is perhaps quite fitting for one who is about to make the journey thither to inquire about the journey to that bourne, and to represent in myth what we believe concerning it. Indeed, what else could one do in the time between now and sunset?' [7]

[CEBES.]   'What right have they to say, Socrates, that a man is not to kill himself? I did, in fact, on the point you just now asked about, hear Philolaus say while he was staying with us, and have heard others also say, that it was something one should not do. But from no one have I ever heard anything precise about these matters.'

62 [SOCRATES.]   'Courage!' he said. 'Possibly you are going to hear it, though probably, when you do, you may think it strange, and wonder if this rule alone, among all others, has no exception, and if with mankind it never happens, as in all else, that there are occasions when, and persons for whom, it is better to die than live. And if there are persons for whom death is better, it may seem strange to you if for these men it is a wicked act to give themselves the benefit, and instead they must wait for some one else to be the benefactor.'

[CEBES.]   And Cebes quietly smiled at that, and said 'God wot!'— using his native phrase.

[SOCRATES.]   'And there would seem,' said Socrates, 'to be something irrational in that. However, there is not; rather, there is probably some ground for it. What is said of this matter in the Mysteries, namely that "we men are under guard, and one must not release oneself therefrom nor run away," sounds grand to me, and quite

[7] The legal hour for execution.

easy to see through. On the other hand, this, Cebes, seems to me well said, that there are gods, and they have us in charge, and that we men are one of the possessions of the gods. Does it not seem so to you?'

[CEBES.] 'It does indeed,' said Cebes.

[SOCRATES.] 'Well now,' said he, 'suppose that one of your possessions [e. g., a slave] killed itself without your signifying that you wished to have it die; would you be angry with it? And if you had the means of taking vengeance on it, would you do so?'

[CEBES.] 'Indeed I would,' he said.

[SOCRATES.] 'Then probably in that sense it is not irrational to hold that one must never kill oneself before God sends a summons of necessity; one must await a call like this which is here for us to-day.'

[CEBES.] 'Yes,' said Cebes, 'that sounds right enough. But what you just now said, about philosophers being ready to die, that, Socrates, looks quite incredible, if what we just now said holds good, that the Deity is watching over us, and we are His possessions. That the most intelligent of men should not be grieved to pass out from this care, in which they have as rulers over them the best there are, the gods, does not make sense. Surely no such man will think it better that, through the gain of his freedom, he should have himself in his own charge. Perhaps a senseless man might have these notions, might think that one should flee from one's lord, and might not reflect that a man ought not to do it, at least when his lord is good, but ought above all to abide with him. The flight in that case would proceed from a want of reason. But surely the man of sense would desire to be always with his better. Consequently, Socrates, the likely thing is the opposite of what was just now said; it is proper for the wise to grieve at dying, and for senseless men to be glad.'

[SOCRATES.] On hearing that, Socrates was gratified, I thought, at Cebes' vigorous procedure, and, turning to us, remarked: 'Really, 63 Cebes always follows out some line of argument, and will not at all readily accept what any one asserts.'

[SIMMIAS.] And Simmias replied: 'But, Socrates, this time Cebes seems to me as well to be making an important point. Why indeed should men who are truly wise desire to escape from masters better than themselves, and lightly to depart from them? And it seems to me that Cebes is aiming his argument at you because you can so lightly bear to leave both us and rulers you yourself admit to be good, the gods.'

[SOCRATES.] 'You are right,' said he; 'for I think you mean that I must defend myself against these charges as if I were in court.'

[SIMMIAS.] 'Indeed you must,' said Simmias.

[SOCRATES.] 'Come now,' said he; 'I will endeavor to defend myself more effectively to you than to the judges; for, Simmias and Cebes,' he said, 'if I did not think I was to go, first, to other gods both wise and good, and, next, to men departed who were better than those here, I should be wrong in not being grieved at death. As it is, you may rest assured, I expect to meet with men who are good; and if I cannot positively aver that, yet that I shall come to gods as rulers who are good—be assured that, if I can be positive on any question of the sort, I am positive on this. So that is why I am not troubled to the same extent [as if there were no hope]. No, I have good hope that there is something after death, and that, as is said from of old, it is far better for the good than for the bad.'

[SIMMIAS.] 'What of it, Socrates?' said Simmias. 'Will you keep this view to yourself now that you are minded to depart, or will you share it with us? To me, this thing would seem to be a good in common for us all; and withal you will make good your defence, if what you say convinces us.'

[SOCRATES.] 'Well then, I will try,' said he. 'But first let us see what it is our Crito here seems all this while to be wanting to tell me.'

[CRITO.] 'Why, Socrates, simply this,' said Crito; 'it is what the man who is to give you the poison said to me some time ago—that you must be told to talk as little as may be. He says that people get warmed up more in discussion, and that nothing of the sort must be allowed to hinder the poison. Otherwise sometimes people who do the like are forced to take a second dose, or even a third.'

[SOCRATES.] 'Don't let him bother you,' said he. 'All he has to do is to be ready to give it twice, if need be, or even thrice.'

[CRITO.] 'Pretty much what I was thinking,' replied Crito, 'but he has been bothering me all this while.'

[SOCRATES.] 'Never mind,' said he. 'But now to you who are my judges let me duly give the reason why it appears quite natural to me that a man who verily has spent his life in philosophy should be of good cheer when he is about to die, and hopeful that there 64 below he will obtain the greatest good when life has ended. How this can be so, Simmias and Cebes, I will endeavor to explain.

'Whoever devotes himself to philosophy in proper fashion is likely to be misunderstood by everybody else; men do not see that all his business is to die or to be dead. If, now, this really is his occupation, surely it would be strange for him all through his life to yearn for this one thing, and it alone, and then, when it came, to be grieved at what of yore he longed for and rehearsed.'

[SIMMIAS.] And Simmias laughed. 'By Heaven! Socrates,' he said, 'just now I was in anything but a mood for laughing, but you have made me do it. When the crowd heard any one say that, they would think that it was very well directed at the people who pursue philosophy; and the men where I live would join with them in complete assent that, absolutely, people who pursue philosophy are ripe for death, nor would they fail to recognize this lot as well deserved.'

[SOCRATES.] 'And, Simmias, they would be right in saying so, apart from what they do not "fail to recognize"; they do not, in fact, see in what way true philosophers are ripe for death, or worthy of it, nor of what sort of death. Indeed, we must discuss the matter for ourselves, without attention to the crowd.

'Do we consider death as something?'

[SIMMIAS.] 'Yes, certainly,' said Simmias in reply.

[SOCRATES.] 'Can it be anything else than a separation of the spirit from the body? And to be dead is this: the body parted from the spirit, and separate, is isolated in itself, and the spirit parted from the body, and separate, is isolated in itself? Death is nothing else than that?'

[SIMMIAS.] 'No, it is just that,' said he.

[SOCRATES.] 'Consider, now, good friend; see if perchance you share my views; for from these I think we can better understand the object of our search. Does it seem to you the part of a philosopher to be concerned about such so-called pleasures as the following—eating and drinking, for example?'

[SIMMIAS.] 'As little, Socrates, as he can,' said Simmias.

[SOCRATES.] 'What about venereal pleasures?'

[SIMMIAS.] 'Absolutely not.'

[SOCRATES.] 'What about the care of the body otherwise? Do you think that such a man will greatly value it? Take, for example, getting superior clothes and shoes and all other efforts to adorn the body; do you think that he will value clothes and so on much beyond the point where absolute necessity compels one to secure them?'

[SIMMIAS.] 'I think, for my part, he will set small value on them, in so far as he is truly philosophic.'

[SOCRATES.] 'On the whole, then, does it seem to you,' said he, 'that the concern of such a man will not be with the body, but as far as he is able to detach himself from this, will be directed to the spirit?'

[SIMMIAS.] 'Yes.'

[SOCRATES.] 'Well then, to begin with. is the philosopher revealed in
65 some such point as this, that he, beyond all other men, will free the spirit to the utmost from communion with the body?'

[SIMMIAS.] 'Clearly yes.'

[SOCRATES.] 'And, Simmias, no doubt it seems to the majority of men that any one for whom such pleasures have no meaning, and who does not partake of them, is unfit to be alive; rather, that he who thinks nothing of those pleasures that come by way of the body runs close to being dead?'

[SIMMIAS.] 'What you say is altogether true.'

[SOCRATES.] 'What, now, about the actual attainment of intelligence? Is the body an impediment, or not, if one takes it along conjointly in the quest? The sort of thing I mean is this. Do sight and hearing, both, furnish men with some degree of truth? Or is it as the poets are for ever telling us, that nothing do we see, and nothing hear, distinctly? And if, among the bodily sensations, these are indistinct and no way certain, the others hardly count, being all of them, no doubt, inferior to these. Is n't that your view?'

[SIMMIAS.] 'Indeed it is,' said he.

[SOCRATES.] 'Then when,' said he, 'does the soul attain to the truth? When it tries to study something with the aid of the body, obviously it will be misled by this.'

[SIMMIAS.] 'That is true.'

[SOCRATES.] 'Well then, will it not be in the act of reasoning, if ever anywhere, that the reality of something is made manifest to her?'

[SIMMIAS.] 'Yes.'

[SOCRATES.] 'But no doubt she reasons best at a time when none of these things disturbs her, neither hearing, nor sight, nor pain, nor any pleasure; when, rather, being in the utmost isolation, dismissing the body, and, as far as she is able, having no communion and no contact with it, she reaches after true reality.'

[SIMMIAS.] 'So it is.'

[SOCRATES.] 'So in this case too the soul of the philosopher slights the body to the last degree, and flees from it, and seeks to be herself alone?'

[SIMMIAS.] 'That is clear.'

[SOCRATES.] 'What about such points as follow, Simmias? Do we say there is in essence such a thing as "just," or do we not?'

[SIMMIAS.] 'By Heaven, we do affirm it, yes!'

[SOCRATES.] 'And also such a thing as "beautiful," and "good"?'

[SIMMIAS.] 'Of course.'

[SOCRATES.] 'Now did you ever see a thing like any of them with your eyes?'

[SIMMIAS.] 'Never,' he replied.

[SOCRATES.] 'Well, do we grasp them through some other sense of those that operate through the body? I am speaking of all cases, such as magnitude, health, strength, and, in a word, of the reality of all the rest—speaking of what each really is. Is it through the body that their highest truth is seen? Or is it thus?—that he among us who most thoroughly and keenly gives himself to contemplation of the individual object, in itself, which he investigates, he it is who will come closest to a knowledge of it?'

[SIMMIAS.] 'Most certainly.'

[SOCRATES.] 'Then would not he do this most purely who most used reason alone in going to the individual thing, taking no account of

66   sight or any other sense in the act of thinking, nor yoking any one
      of them with reason? He who, rather, employing pure thought in
      and by itself, undertakes to hunt the individual reality itself, pure
      and simple, by itself, winning free as far as anybody can from eyes
      and ears and, so to speak, the body, all of it, as something that dis-
      turbs the soul, and, when conjoined with her, keeps her from ac-
      quiring truth and wisdom? Is not this man, Simmias, the one who,
      if ever anybody does it, will hit upon reality?'

[SIMMIAS.]   'How admirably, Socrates,' said Simmias, 'you state the
      truth!'

[SOCRATES.]   'Accordingly,' said he, 'from all these premises, there
      is perforce brought home to genuine philosophers some such belief
      as follows, and so they say to one another things like these:

      ' "It seems as if there were a kind of path that led us on the trail
      when we search in company with reason; for while we have the
      body, and our spirit is mingled with that evil thing, we shall never
      adequately possess what we desire—and this object we declare to
      be truth; for not only does the body bring untold distractions upon
      us because of the necessities of life, but in addition various diseases
      may befall us to impede our hunting for reality. Loves, desires, and
      fears, imaginations of all sorts, much vanity, the body fills us with
      them till (as the saying truly goes) because of it we actually never
      get the chance to think one single thought. Yes, it is the body and
      its desires, nought else, that brings on wars, dissensions, and fight-
      ing; for all the wars are brought about on account of money-
      making, and we are forced to get the money because of the body
      and our slavery to its service. And from it we get the want of leisure
      for philosophy because of all these things. But worst of all, if we
      at length find any interval of freedom from it, and turn to studying
      a thing, again at every point in our researches the body bobs up to
      interrupt and trouble us, and dazes us, so that because of it we can-
      not perceive the truth. But the fact is we have had it proved to us
      that if ever we are going to obtain pure knowledge, we must get
      away from the body, and with the soul itself see things themselves.
      And then, it would seem, we shall have that which we desire, that
      which we say we are in love with, wisdom; we shall have it when

we are departed, so signifies the argument, and not while we are living; for if it is impossible to have pure knowledge of anything whatsoever with the body present, there are two alternatives. Either we never can attain to knowledge, or we can attain it only after death; for then the soul will be alone and by itself, without the body, and before that it will not. And, while we are alive, it seems that the nearest we can come to knowing is by having as far as possible no association nor communion with the body, more than absolute necessity demands, nor suffering the contagion of its nature, but remaining uncontaminated by it until God himself shall release us. And thus, pure, emancipated from the unreason of the body, it is probable we shall join with beings of like nature, and through our inmost selves know all the pure reality. And this no doubt is truth; for to impurity we fear it is not granted to lay hold on what is pure."

'There, Simmias, I think we have the sort of thing that all right lovers of learning must needs tell one another and believe. Does it not seem so to you?'

[SIMMIAS.] 'Yes, Socrates, beyond all doubt.'

[SOCRATES.] 'Well then, my dear friend,' said Socrates, 'if that is true, great is the hope for him who has reached the place where I am going, that there if anywhere he will have abundantly that for which we have taken so much trouble in the life gone by; so that this migration which is now enjoined on me is attended with good hope for anybody else who deems that his mind is purified and therefore ready.'

[SIMMIAS.] 'Absolutely right,' said Simmias.

[SOCRATES.] 'But does not purgation [*catharsis*] mean this, as stated in the argument before, the utmost separation of the spirit from the body? And to collect and rally herself at all points from the body, and to dwell, as far as possible, both here and now and in the time to come, alone and by herself, released from the body as from chains?'

[SIMMIAS.] 'Absolutely right,' said he.

[SOCRATES.] 'Well, and is not death the name for this, just this release and severing of soul from body?'

[SIMMIAS.] 'Just that,' he said.

[SOCRATES.] 'Yes, and that release, so we affirmed, is what true lovers of wisdom, and they alone, are always longing for above all else, and the main concern of the philosophers is this very thing, release and severance of soul from body. Is it not?'

[SIMMIAS.] 'That is clear.'

[SOCRATES.] 'Well then, as I said at the outset, would it not be ridiculous if a man in his lifetime set himself to live as nearly as he could to the state of being dead, and then when death came to him he should be grieved at it?'

[SIMMIAS.] 'It would be ridiculous indeed.'

[SOCRATES.] 'So, Simmias,' said he, 'it is the fact that those who rightly follow after wisdom are concerned with dying, and least of all among mankind are they afraid of death. Look at the matter thus. If at every point they spurn the body, and if they wish to have the soul alone and by itself, then, when this comes about, how inconsistent they would be to be afraid of it and grieve, not to go rejoicing thither where when they arrive it is their hope to find what all their life they craved (but what they craved was wisdom!), their hope as well to be rid of being with the thing they spurned? What! for an earthly love—youth or wife or son that died—many a man has freely chosen to go down to Hades in the hope that there he would see and join the object of his longing; and will one who really loves wisdom, and cherishes exceedingly the selfsame hope that he can meet with wisdom worthy of the name in Hades and no other place but that—will he be grieved when he comes to die? Will he not go thither rejoicing? We are bound to think that he will, my friend, if he really is a true philosopher; for he will be extremely firm in the belief that nowhere else will he find knowledge in its purity, but only there. If that is so, would it not be what I just now said, the height of inconsistency for such a man to be afraid of death?'

[SIMMIAS.] 'Yes, by Heaven! the very height of it,' said he.

[SOCRATES.] 'Well,' said he, 'when you see a man aggrieved because he is about to die, is that not evidence enough for you that he is no philosopher, but a lover of the body? And very likely this same man will also be a lover of money and of honors, one or both?'

[SIMMIAS.] 'Certainly,' said he. 'You are quite right.'

[SOCRATES.] 'Now then, Simmias,' he said, 'does not what is known as courage belong especially to persons of the disposition I described?'

[SIMMIAS.] 'Yes, surely,' he replied.

[SOCRATES.] 'And the same is true of temperance—of temperance also in the ordinary sense? That is, with reference to desires to run to no extremes, but to rate them low and hold to moderation? Does not this belong especially to those who slight the body, and live in philosophy?'

[SIMMIAS.] 'Necessarily,' he said.

[SOCRATES.] 'Consider,' said he, 'if you please, the courage and the temperance of all the rest, and you will see their inconsistency.'

[SIMMIAS.] 'In what way, Socrates?'

[SOCRATES.] 'You know,' said he, 'that all the rest think death to be one of the major evils?'

[SIMMIAS.] 'They do indeed,' he said.

[SOCRATES.] 'Well, and when the brave among them go to meet death, they do so out of fear of greater evils?'

[SIMMIAS.] 'That is true.'

[SOCRATES.] 'So all are brave through fearing and for fear save the philosophers. And yet it is irrational for one to be courageous out of fear and cowardice!'

[SIMMIAS.] 'It is indeed.'

[SOCRATES.] 'What about those among them who are temperate? They are in the same condition?—are moderate through a certain lack of moderation? We say it is impossible, yet their condition does turn out to be like that with reference to their shallow kind of temperance. They fear they will lose pleasures they desire, and so abstain from certain pleasures because of others that have them in subjection. It is true they call intemperance the state of being ruled 69 by pleasures, and yet it is a fact that in the course of being dominated by some pleasures they get the mastery of others. That is like the statement made just now, that in a way their temperance is effected through intemperance?'

[SIMMIAS.] 'So it seems.'

[SOCRATES.] 'My noble Simmias, with respect to virtue, that is hardly the right standard of exchange, to balance pleasure against pleasure, pain with pain, and fear with fear, the greater of them with the less, as if you were exchanging money. But perhaps that is the true coin only, in exchange for which you must give all these pains and pleasures, namely wisdom. And possibly for and with this coin all things in reality are bought and sold—this and courage, temperance, and justice—in a word, true virtue joined with wisdom, whether pleasures, pains, and all else of the sort be present or be absent. If these things are divorced from wisdom, and given in exchange for one another, this kind of virtue may be but a shadow-image, a virtue really servile, with never an atom of health or truth. The truth may really be a purging away of all these things, conjoint with temperance, justice, and courage; and wisdom itself may be simply a purgation. And it is possible as well that they who founded the Mysteries for us are not to be despised, but in reality their ancient riddle means that he who reaches Hades uninitiated and imperfect will lie in the Slough, while he who has been cleansed and is perfected will, on his arrival there, have his dwelling-place with gods; for, as they who have to do with the initiations put it:

Many bear the thyrsus, but few are the inspired.

These last, to my mind, are no other than those who have pursued philosophy in the proper sense; to be one of whom I too, according to my power, have in my life left naught undone, but in every way have done my best. Whether my effort has been right, and we have been at all successful, once we are there we shall, God willing, a little later know for certain. Or such is my opinion.

'There,' he said, 'my Simmias and Cebes, is my defence, the reason why in leaving you, and my masters here as well, I do not take it hard nor grieve, for I think that there as here I shall meet with masters that are good, and with good companions. The crowd will not believe it. Accordingly, if to you I am somewhat more convincing in my defence than I was to the Athenian judges, it is well.'

[PHAEDO.]   When Socrates had spoken thus, Cebes rejoined:

[CEBES.]   'To me, all that seems well put, Socrates, save for the part
about the soul; that part must excite great incredulity among man-   70
kind. People believe that when the soul is severed from the body,
it no longer has existence anywhere, but, on the day when the man
dies, it perishes and is destroyed; the moment it is severed from the
body, dissipated like a breath or smoke it vanishes, and is nothing
anywhere thereafter. And so if in reality it were somewhere re-
united in itself, and released from those evils which you just now
listed, how great and lovely, Socrates, would be the hope that what
you say is true! But doubtless it calls for not a little reassuring argument, and for proof, to make one hold that, when the man is dead,
the soul exists and has activity and intelligence.'

[SOCRATES.]   'Right, Cebes,' answered Socrates. 'But what are we to
do? Is it your wish that we go through the story of these matters,
and see if it is likely they are so or not?'

[CEBES.]   'For my part,' answered Cebes, 'I would gladly hear what
view you take concerning them.'

[SOCRATES.]   'Well then,' said Socrates, 'I do not think that any one
who listened to me now, not even if he were a comic poet, would
say that I was garrulous and talked of matters that did not concern
me. If you wish it, then, the subject must be thoroughly examined.

'Let us look at it in some such way as this. The souls of the people
who have died, are they in Hades or are they not? Well, there is
an ancient doctrine, to which we have referred, that there below
are they who came from here, and that they do in fact come back
again and are here reborn from those who have died. And if this
actually is so, if the living are reborn from those who die, can it be
otherwise than that our spirits must be there? Did they not exist,
doubtless they could not be born again; and it is proof enough of
their existence if it can in fact be shown that the living cannot come
from any other source whatever save the dead. If that is not the case,
however, then some other argument is needed.'

[CEBES.]   'That is quite certain,' answered Cebes.

[SOCRATES.]   'Now then,' he continued, 'if you wish to understand this thing more readily, do not look at it simply with respect to men; no, consider it with reference to all animals and plants as well, and, taking comprehensively all things that have a birth, let us see if in all cases everything does not arise in this way, namely, that opposites proceed from nothing else save opposites, wherever a relation of such sort obtains; as, for instance, the beautiful, I take it, is in opposition with the ugly, right with wrong, and, naturally, the relation holds in countless other cases. So let us look into this, and see if, necessarily, whenever anything has something opposite to it, it issues from no other source but that, its opposite, and that alone. For example, when something becomes greater, then necessarily, no doubt, it is out of something previously smaller that it comes to be so?'

[CEBES.] 'Yes.'

[SOCRATES.] 'Well, and if a thing grows smaller, it will become so later out of something that before was greater?'

71

[CEBES.] 'So it is,' said he.

[SOCRATES.] 'And just so the weaker from the stronger, and the swifter from the slower?'

[CEBES.] 'Yes indeed.'

[SOCRATES.] 'Further, if a thing grows worse, it will do so from a better, and if juster, from a more unjust?'

[CEBES.] 'That is certain.'

[SOCRATES.] 'Enough,' said he; 'we have this principle, that all things thus arise, the opposites from their opposites.'

[CEBES.] 'Yes indeed.'

[SOCRATES.] 'But again, in these cases is there not some such relation as the following? Between every pair of opposites are there not two processes of generation, one from A to B, and the other back from B to A? Between a greater and a less are increase and diminution, and so we say in one case that the thing increases, and that in the other it decreases?'

[CEBES.] 'Yes,' he said.

[SOCRATES.] 'And so with separating and combining, growing cold and growing hot, and all the like, even if at times we have no terms for them, still this actual relation must exist, that opposites are en-

gendered from each other, and their genesis is the passing of each
into the other.'

[CEBES.] 'Yes indeed,' said he.

[SOCRATES.] 'What follows, then?' he rejoined. 'Is there something
that is opposite to living, as waking is the opposite of sleeping?'

[CEBES.] 'Most certainly there is,' said he.

[SOCRATES.] 'What?'

[CEBES.] 'Being dead,' he answered.

[SOCRATES.] 'And therefore, if these things are real opposites, then
each arises from the other, and, as they are two, so also are the
intervening processes of generation two.'

[CEBES.] 'That is certain.'

[SOCRATES.] 'Now then,' said Socrates, 'of the opposites I spoke about
a moment ago, I will name one pair to you, the pair together with
its dual generation; and you shall name the other pair to me. I
mention, on the one hand, sleeping, on the other, being awake, and
say that being awake arises out of sleeping, sleeping out of being
awake, and that the processes for them are, on the one hand, falling asleep, on the other, waking up. Does that content you,' said
he, 'or does it not?'

[CEBES.] 'Perfectly.'

[SOCRATES.] 'Now, you tell me, on your part,' said he, 'in like manner
about life and death. Do you not maintain that to be dead is the
opposite of living?'

[CEBES.] 'I do.'

[SOCRATES.] 'And that each arises from the other?'

[CEBES.] 'Yes.'

[SOCRATES.] 'Then what is it that arises from the living?'

[CEBES.] 'The dead,' said he.

[SOCRATES.] 'And what,' he said, 'arises from the dead?'

[CEBES.] 'One must perforce admit,' said he, 'it is the living.'

[SOCRATES.] 'It is, then, Cebes, from the dead [in the plural number]
that living things are born, and living creatures?'

[CEBES.] 'That is clear,' he said.

[SOCRATES.] 'So it is true,' said he, 'that our souls exist in Hades?'

[CEBES.] 'It would seem so.'

[SOCRATES.] 'Well, and of the two processes that occur with reference to these two opposites, the one, at least, is unmistakable?—for
what is meant by dying, I suppose, is clear, is it not?'

[CEBES.] 'Most certainly.'

[SOCRATES.] 'Then what are we to do?' said he. 'Are we not to
balance it with the opposing process, or is nature on this side lame?
Rather must we not grant to dying some process opposite to it?'

[CEBES.] 'I fancy it must certainly be granted.'

[SOCRATES.] 'What process will this be?'

[CEBES.] 'Coming to life again.'

[SOCRATES.] 'Now then,' said he, 'if there really is a process of
72   revival, must not this process be a generation from the dead towards
the living?'

[CEBES.] 'Yes, certainly.'

[SOCRATES.] 'Then we are agreed on this point also, that the living
come from the dead no whit less than the dead come from the
living. That being so, we would seem to have sufficient proof that
the souls of the dead perforce are in a place from which they can
be born again.'

[CEBES.] 'To my mind, Socrates,' he said, 'from all we have admitted, it must perforce be so.'

[SOCRATES.] 'Well now, look at the matter this way, Cebes,' he continued, 'for a proof, as it seems to me, that we did not come to
an agreement wrongly, either. Suppose there were not an eternal
balance between one thing and another in their generation, a revolution in a circle as it were; suppose there were a genesis straight
forward from a given thing only into that precisely opposite to
it, and no return again into the given thing for a conversion: you
must see that everything would end in uniformity, all things would
undergo the same experience, and there would be no further generation.'

[CEBES.] 'How do you mean?' said he.

[SOCRATES.] 'There is no difficulty,' he replied, 'in grasping what
I mean. Suppose, instead, there were such a thing as falling ásleep,
but that to balance it there were no awaking that issued out of
sleep: you must see that everything would finally make Endymion

[in his endless sleep] quite insignificant, and he would nowhere be observed, for all things else would undergo the same experience as he, and be asleep! And suppose that everything came together, and never separated, the word of Anaxagoras would shortly come to pass: "All things massed together!" Similarly, dear Cebes, were all things that have part in life to die, and, once they died, the dead continued in this state, and did not come to life again, then, quite necessarily, would not all things finally be dead, and nothing be alive? Suppose, in fact, that living creatures come from any other source, but that the living die, is there any possible way by which all things shall not be swallowed up in death?'

[CEBES.] 'No way whatever, Socrates,' said Cebes, 'so far as I can see. No, I think that what you say is absolutely true.'

[SOCRATES.] 'Yes, Cebes,' he said, 'as it seems to me, there is nothing more true than that, and we were not deceived about the premises we agreed on. No; and verily there is a return to life, the living do come from the dead, the spirits of the dead do actually exist, and for the good there is indeed a better lot, a worse one for the bad.'

[CEBES.] 'And surely, Socrates,' said Cebes in return, 'this tallies with that argument, if the latter is sound, which you have often used, that our learning is nothing else than reminiscence; and accordingly we must perforce have learned in some preceding time the things of which we now are reminded. But this would be impossible if our soul had not existed somewhere before its generation in this present human frame. Consequently in this manner too 73 the soul appears to be a thing immortal.'

[SIMMIAS.] 'But, Cebes,' Simmias retorted, 'what kind of evidence is there of this? Do you remind me, for at the moment I do not recall the procedure too well.'

[CEBES.] 'One argument there is,' said Cebes, 'of the finest order. When people are questioned, if you put the questions nicely, of themselves they tell you everything precisely as it is. Well now, if there were no knowledge dwelling in them, and no proper understanding, they would be incapable of doing this. Further, when you come to geometric figures, or anything else of the sort, there you have the clearest evidence that the thing is so.'

[SOCRATES.] 'Quite possibly, Simmias,' said Socrates, 'you will not be convinced by that procedure. If so, see if you agree with me when you look at the matter in some such way as this. You actually are in doubt how that which is called learning is a reminiscence?'

[SIMMIAS.] 'No,' answered Simmias, 'for my part I am not in doubt. But I do need to have done to me the very thing we are discussing; I need to be reminded. And to some extent I already am reminded and convinced by the argument as Cebes tried to give it; all the same I should now be glad to listen to the argument in the way in which you gave it.'

[SOCRATES.] 'My way is this,' said he. 'We are doubtless in agreement that when any one remembers anything, he must at some time previous have known it.'

[SIMMIAS.] 'Yes, certainly,' he said.

[SOCRATES.] 'And so we are agreed on this point too, that whenever knowledge comes to pass under such conditions as the following, it is reminiscence? I mean a case like this. Suppose one hears or sees some thing, or has some other perception, and does not merely know that thing, but thinks of something else as well, something not connoted by that knowledge, but apart from it; then are we not correct in saying that he is reminded of this thing of which he has thought?'

[SIMMIAS.] 'What do you mean?'

[SOCRATES.] 'Cases like the following. Knowledge of a man and of a lyre, I take it, are not the same idea.'

[SIMMIAS.] 'Certainly not.'

[SOCRATES.] 'Well then, are you not aware that lovers when they see a lyre, or a cloak, or anything else their favorites are wont to use, have this experience?—they know the lyre, and therewithal in thought get the image of the boy whose lyre it is? Now that is reminiscence. In the same way, anybody who sees Simmias will often think of Cebes; and no doubt there would be countless other cases of the sort.'

[SIMMIAS.] 'By Heaven, yes!' said Simmias, 'they are countless.'

[SOCRATES.] 'And so,' said he, 'that sort of thing is a reminiscence? But is it not particularly true when any one has this experience with regard to things which time and inattention have led one to forget?'

[SIMMIAS.] 'Yes, certainly,' he said.

[SOCRATES.] 'Come now,' said he. 'When one sees a painting of a horse or of a lyre, is it possible to be reminded of a man, and when one sees a painting of Simmias, to be reminded of Cebes?'

[SIMMIAS.] 'Certainly.'

[SOCRATES.] 'And also when one sees a painting of Simmias, to be reminded of the real Simmias?'

[SIMMIAS.] 'It is indeed,' said he.   74

[SOCRATES.] 'So the fact in all these cases is that the reminiscence sometimes comes from something similar, sometimes, again, from something different?'

[SIMMIAS.] 'Yes, it does.'

[SOCRATES.] 'But take the case in which the reminiscence starts from something similar. Must one not in addition have the following experience of thinking whether this given object lacks to some extent, or does not lack, in similarity to the thing of which one has the reminiscence?'

[SIMMIAS.] 'One must,' he said.

[SOCRATES.] 'Look now,' said he, 'and see if the matter stands thus. I take it there is something we call equal, not as block to block, or stone to stone, or anything like that, but something other than all these, a thing distinct, equality itself. Do we affirm this to be anything, or nothing?'

[SIMMIAS.] 'By Heaven!' Simmias replied, 'we do affirm it to be something. Most decidedly!'

[SOCRATES.] 'And do we know what this thing in its essence is?'

[SIMMIAS.] 'Yes, certainly,' he said.

[SOCRATES.] 'And whence do we derive our knowledge of it? We do not get it, do we, from the things we just now mentioned? When we look at blocks or stones or other things like that, and see that they are equal, we do not get this notion out of them, since it is something different from them? Or does it not appear to you to be a thing distinct? But look at it, again, this way. Do not stones and blocks sometimes, while still the same, appear to one man to be equal, to another not?'

[SIMMIAS.] 'Most certainly.'

[SOCRATES.] 'Come now. Are there cases where the equal has appeared to you to be unequal, or equality to be inequality?'

[SIMMIAS.] 'No, never, Socrates.'

[SOCRATES.] 'And so,' said he, 'these two are not the same: that certain things are equal, and the equal in itself.'

[SIMMIAS.] 'No, Socrates, it is quite clear to me that they are not the same.'

[SOCRATES.] 'And yet,' said he, 'it is from these equal things, which are distinct from the aforesaid "equal," that you conceived and got the knowledge of it.'

[SIMMIAS.] 'You are absolutely right,' he said.

[SOCRATES.] 'And that holds true whether it be like them or unlike them?'

[SIMMIAS.] 'Yes, certainly.'

[SOCRATES.] 'Indeed,' said he, 'it makes no difference at all; the moment you see one thing, and from this perception come to think about another, whether it be similar or different, what comes to pass,' he said, 'is necessarily a reminiscence.'

[SIMMIAS.] 'Most certainly.'

[SOCRATES.] 'But come,' said he. 'Do we have some such experience as the following with respect to the equalities in blocks of wood and in the other things we just now mentioned? Do they present themselves to us as equal in the way the equal in itself does? Do they fall short of it at all, or do they not, in being equal in the way that it is?'

[SIMMIAS.] 'They fall far short of it indeed,' he said.

[SOCRATES.] 'Then are we not agreed on this? When anybody sees a thing, and thinks, "This thing I am now looking at would seem to be like something else, like one of the realities, but fails, and cannot match it, but is an inferior thing," then necessarily, no doubt, the one who has this thought must previously have known this second thing to which he says the first has a resemblance while falling short of it.'

[SIMMIAS.] 'Necessarily.'

[SOCRATES.] 'What then? We too, have we experienced the like, or have we not, with reference to equal things and the equal in itself?'

[SIMMIAS.] 'By all means yes.'

[SOCRATES.] 'So, necessarily, we must have previously known the equal before the time when first we saw the equal things, and had the thought that all these things seek to be like the equal, but fall short of it.' 75

[SIMMIAS.] 'So it is.'

[SOCRATES.] 'But here is another point on which we are agreed. This thought would not have come about, nor could one have the thought, if one began from any other source save sight or touch or another of the sensory perceptions; I reckon all these as the same.'

[SIMMIAS.] 'In any case they are the same, Socrates, for what the argument seeks to prove.'

[SOCRATES.] 'Well, at all events from sensory perceptions we must derive the thought that all the sensible equalities seek after that equality which is real, and fall short of it. Or what do we say?'

[SIMMIAS.] 'That!'

[SOCRATES.] 'And so, before we begin to see and hear and have the rest of the sensations, we must somehow have got a knowledge of the equal in itself, the true reality; that is, if we are going to refer thereto the equalities drawn from sensory perceptions, and to think that all such seek to be like that, but are inferior to it.'

[SIMMIAS.] 'That follows necessarily, Socrates, from what has gone before.'

[SOCRATES.] 'As soon as we were born, immediately we saw and heard and had the rest of the sensations?'

[SIMMIAS.] 'Yes, certainly.'

[SOCRATES.] 'And in advance of these, we say, we necessarily had got a knowledge of the equal?'

[SIMMIAS.] 'Yes.'

[SOCRATES.] 'And so we must have got it, seemingly, before we were born.'

[SIMMIAS.] 'So it seems.'

[SOCRATES.] 'Accordingly, if, having got it before our birth, we were born possessed of it; then both before our birth, and as soon as we were born, we would have a knowledge not only of the equal, and the greater and the less, but of all the like ideas, every one of them, as well, would we not? For now, in fact, our argument does not concern the equal any more than it concerns the beautiful *per se*, and the good, the just, and the holy *per se*, and universally, as I express it, all the concepts upon which in all our questions when we ask, and all our answers in replying, we put the seal "Reality itself." And so, perforce, we must have got the knowledge of all these before our birth.'

[SIMMIAS.] 'That is true.'

[SOCRATES.] 'And suppose that, having got it, we did not on each occasion [of rebirth] forget it, then, every time, we would perforce be born aware of it, and would know it, every time, throughout our life; for knowing consists in this, namely, after getting knowledge of a thing, to hold and not to lose it. Or by "forgetting," Simmias, do we not mean the loss of knowledge?'

[SIMMIAS.] 'No doubt of it whatever, Socrates,' he said.

[SOCRATES.] 'But if, methinks, having got it before birth, and lost it when we were born, yet later when we use our senses with regard to those ideas we regain the former knowledge of them which we once possessed; then would not what we call learning be regaining knowledge which was ours? But if we called this "reminiscence," no doubt we should be giving it its rightful name?'

[SIMMIAS.] 'Yes, certainly.'

76 [SOCRATES.] 'It is possible, in fact, or so it seems, that in perceiving anything by sight or hearing, or by any other of the senses, we are led from it to think of something which we had forgotten, with which the first stands in relation, whether unlike or like it being immaterial. And so, I say, you have one of two alternatives. Either we are born with a knowledge of the said realities, and everybody knows them all his life; or, after they are born, those who, as we say, "learn," do nothing else than recollect, and in that case learning must be reminiscence.'

[SIMMIAS.] 'Yes, Socrates, that certainly must be the way things stand.'

[SOCRATES.] 'Then which alternative, Simmias, do you take? We are born possessed of knowledge, or we later recollect the things of which we formerly gained the knowledge?'

[SIMMIAS.] 'At the moment, Socrates, I cannot decide.'

[SOCRATES.] 'Well then! You can decide the point that follows, and tell me what you think of it. A man who knows about a thing, is he able, or unable, to give a rational account of what he knows?'

[SIMMIAS.] 'He surely must be able, Socrates,' said he.

[SOCRATES.] 'Well, and do you think that every one can give a rational explanation of the things concerning which we just now spoke?'

[SIMMIAS.] 'Ah! would that it were so,' said Simmias. 'But far more I fear that at this hour to-morrow no living man will any more be able worthily to do it.'

[SOCRATES.] 'Consequently, Simmias, it is your view that everybody does not have a knowledge of the said realities?'

[SIMMIAS.] 'Absolutely not!'

[SOCRATES.] 'And so they recollect what once they learned?'

[SIMMIAS.] 'Necessarily.'

[SOCRATES.] 'When was it that our souls got a knowledge of these things? Surely it was not when we were born as men.'

[SIMMIAS.] 'Surely not.'

[SOCRATES.] 'So it must have been before?'

[SIMMIAS.] 'Yes.'

[SOCRATES.] 'So, Simmias, our spirits, before they were in human shape, existed, without bodies, and possessed intelligence?'

[SIMMIAS.] 'Yes, Socrates, unless we got this knowledge at the time when we were born, for this time still remains a possibility.'

[SOCRATES.] 'Eh, friend? Then at what other time, pray, did we lose it? A little while ago we were agreed that we do not come into the world possessed of it. Or do we lose it at the very moment when we get it? Or have you any other time to offer?'

[SIMMIAS.] 'None whatever, Socrates. Nor did I see that what I said was nothing to the purpose.'

[SOCRATES.] 'Are we not, then, Simmias, in this position? If the things that we keep talking of exist, the good, the beautiful, and all the like reality; if we refer all sensory perceptions to that as something pre-existent which we find to be our own; and if we bring these things into comparison with that reality; then, by the same necessity which governs the existence of all that, our spirit also must exist before our birth. If such is not the case, this argument will go for nothing, will it not? Is not that how matters stand? And the necessity is equal for these things to have existence and for our souls to have existence before we are born; and equal for the non-existence of the one and the non-existence of the other?'

[SIMMIAS.] 'Beyond all question, Socrates,' said Simmias, 'there seems to me to be the same necessity; and the argument [we are pursuing] has finely run to cover in the parallel between the existence of our soul before our birth and the existence of that reality which you just now mentioned. For me no other argument could be equally convincing. Everything of this description has the highest title to existence—beauty, goodness, and all the other things you just now mentioned. And for me the demonstration is sufficient.'

77

[SOCRATES.] 'But what about Cebes now?' said Socrates. 'Cebes also has to be convinced.'

[SIMMIAS.] 'He is content,' said Simmias, 'or so I fancy; although he is the stiffest person in the world in his distrust of any argument. He does not, however, need to be convinced of this, I think, that our soul existed before we were born. But whether it will still exist when we are dead, that, Socrates,' he said, 'not even I myself believe has yet been proved. No, the difficulty still remains which Cebes just now raised, the general fear that with his death the spirit of the man is dissipated, and that this marks the end of its existence. What, actually, could keep it from arising and combining from some other source [than Hades], from formerly existing in a human body, and, after it arrived there and was separated thence, then coming to an end and perishing?'

[CEBES.] 'Well spoken, Simmias,' said Cebes. 'Clearly, as it were, a half of what is called for has been proved—that our soul was in existence before our birth. In addition, one must prove as well that after we are dead it will exist no less than before we were born, if the demonstration is to reach its goal.'

[SOCRATES.] 'It is already demonstrated, Simmias and Cebes,' said Socrates, 'if you will join in one this argument and that which we accepted before this, that every living thing arises from the dead; for if the soul exists before, but necessarily, when it comes into living and is born, can come from no source other than from death and being dead, what can the necessary consequence be but that it must exist as well when one is dead, since it must once again be born? Accordingly, the point you mention has been proved as matters stand.

'And yet it looks to me as if both you and Simmias would be glad to argue this question out more thoroughly; and as if you entertained the childish fear that, verily, at the moment when the soul departed from the body the wind dispersed and dissipated it, above all if one did not chance to die when the air was calm, but in a heavy gale!'

[CEBES.]   And Cebes, laughing, said: 'Try giving a persuasive argument for cowards, Socrates; not so much, though, as if we were fearful, but rather as if there actually were still within us a child who feared such things. Take him, and try to change his mind, persuading him not to be afraid of death as of a bugbear.'

[SOCRATES.]   'Come!' said Socrates; 'he will have to get an incantation every day, till you have rid him of his fear.'

[CEBES.]   'And whence, then, Socrates,' he said, 'shall we obtain a 78 good enchanter for such fears, now that you,' he said, 'are going to desert us?'

[SOCRATES.]   'Cebes,' he answered, 'Hellas is very large, and no doubt there are good men in it; and, as for the barbarians, there are many tribes of them. You must investigate among all these, and seek such an enchanter, sparing neither money nor effort, on the ground that there is nothing upon which you could more seasonably lay out your wealth. You must seek too by yourselves, together; for quite possibly you would not discover any one more capable of this function than are you.'

[CEBES.] 'Well, this thing shall be attended to,' said Cebes. 'But let us go on again where we left off, if that will please you.'

[SOCRATES.] 'It will indeed. Why think it could be otherwise?'

[CEBES.] 'Very good,' he said.

[SOCRATES.] 'The question that we have to ask ourselves,' said Socrates, 'is something of this order, is it not? What kind of thing is it whose lot it is to suffer this experience, namely, of dispersion, and what kind of thing are we to fear for lest it suffer that, and what kind of thing escapes? And thereafter we must look, again, to see if it is soul or not, and upon these grounds we are to fear or not to fear with regard to our own soul?'

[CEBES.] 'That is right,' he said.

[SOCRATES.] 'And so to what has been compounded, and by nature is composite, it appertains to suffer this, to be divided precisely in the way in which it was composed? Whereas, if something happens not to be composite, to this alone it appertains, if it appertains to anything at all, not to suffer dissolution?'

[CEBES.] 'Yes,' said Cebes, 'that is how matters look to me.'

[SOCRATES.] 'Such things, then, as remain identical with themselves, and are always in the same condition, is it not most likely that they are the uncompounded? Whereas the things that at one time are in one condition, at another in another, never keeping their identity, these are the compounded?'

[CEBES.] 'To my mind, that is so.'

[SOCRATES.] 'Now let us go,' said he, 'to the point to which we went in the preceding argument. That essential reality, of whose being we render account alike in question and reply, what of it? Does it remain identical with itself, or is it now in one condition, now in another? The equal itself, the beautiful itself, what any given thing is in itself, reality, is it ever capable of any change whatever? Or is not each of these realities, being uniform when taken by itself, always in the same condition, and ever, everywhere, in all respects, incapable of any change whatever?'

[CEBES.] 'Yes, Socrates,' he said, 'each must perforce remain unchanged, identical with itself.'

[SOCRATES.] 'But what about the many things of beauty, such as men, horses, garments, or anything else of the sort, things that have the name of equal or of good, or all the other things that share the names of those realities? Do these keep their identity, or, just the opposite of those, is it not the case that they are never constant to themselves or to each other, never, so to say, in any way identical?'

[CEBES.] 'Again,' said Cebes, 'yes; they never remain in the same condition.'

[SOCRATES.] 'And so these you can touch, or see, or apprehend by 79 the other senses; whereas those which keep their own identity it is not possible for you to grasp by any means except the operation of the mind? No, things like these cannot be seen, and are not for the eye.'

[CEBES.] 'What you say,' said he, 'is absolutely right.'

[SOCRATES.] 'Will you let us posit, then,' said he, 'two kinds of things, one visible, the other not?'

[CEBES.] 'Let us posit them,' he said.

[SOCRATES.] 'And we hold that the invisible remains the same, whereas the visible never does?'

[CEBES.] 'We posit that as well,' said he.

[SOCRATES.] 'Come now,' he continued. 'Are we not made up of two things, soul and body?'

[CEBES.] 'Yes, we are,' he said.

[SOCRATES.] 'Then which of the two kinds do we say the body is more like, and to which is it by nature more allied?'

[CEBES.] 'That,' he said, 'is obvious to every one. It is like the visible.'

[SOCRATES.] 'What about the soul? Visible or not?'

[CEBES.] 'Not visible, Socrates,' said he, 'at all events to men.'

[SOCRATES.] 'But when we talk of visible and invisible, we mean with reference to human nature? Or are you thinking of some other nature?'

[CEBES.] 'Human nature.'

[SOCRATES.] 'What, then, do we say about the soul? Can it be seen, or not?'

[CEBES.] 'It can not.'

[SOCRATES.] 'It is, therefore, a thing invisible?'

[CEBES.] 'Yes.'

[SOCRATES.] 'And so the soul is something more like the invisible than is the body, and the latter is a thing more like the seen.'

[CEBES.] 'By all means, Socrates, it must be so.'

[SOCRATES.] 'A while ago we said this also—did we not?—that when the soul employs the body in examining a thing, whether with sight or hearing, or with some other sense (for that is what examining with the body means—examining through the senses); then the soul is by the body drawn to the things that never stay the same, and herself goes wandering, is troubled, and grows dizzy as if drunken, just because she is in contact with such things?'

[CEBES.] 'Yes, certainly.'

[SOCRATES.] 'When, however, she herself contemplates by herself, she is transported yonder to the pure, eternal, deathless, and un-changing essence; and, as being of one kin with it, ever abides with it as oft as she is by herself, and is not hindered; and she ceases from her straying, and, in the company of those realities, ever remains identical with herself, she being in contact with things like that. Is n't it so? And this experience of hers is known as Wisdom?'

[CEBES.] 'Well and truly stated, Socrates,' he said, 'in every way.'

[SOCRATES.] 'So once more, from both our previous and our present argument, which kind of things, in your opinion, is the soul more like and more akin to?'

[CEBES.] 'It seems to me,' he said, 'that everybody, Socrates, even the most dull of wit, must, from this line of argument, concede that totally and in every way the soul has more resemblance to what is always in the same condition than to what is not.'

[SOCRATES.] 'What about the body?'

[CEBES.] 'It has more resemblance to the other kind.'

[SOCRATES.] 'Now look at the matter in another way. When soul and body are together, it is the ordinance of nature that the body shall obey and shall be ruled, and that the soul shall rule and be the master. Then once more, in this relation, which of them seems to you to be more like what is divine, and which more like the mortal? Or does it not seem to you that by nature the divine is fit to rule and to direct, the mortal to be ruled and in subjection?'

[CEBES.] 'To me it does.'

[SOCRATES.] 'Then which of the two does the soul resemble?'

[CEBES.] 'Obviously, Socrates, the soul is like that which is divine, the body like the mortal.'

[SOCRATES.] 'Look, now, Cebes,' he replied, 'and see if the result of all that we have said is not as follows. That which is divine, immortal, of the intellect [noumenal], uniform, incapable of dissolution, and ever in identity with itself, this it is to which the soul has most resemblance; and what is human, mortal, of the senses, multiform, prone to dissolution, and never in identity with itself, this it is, again, which the body most resembles. Have we anything to urge against this view, dear Cebes, any argument to prove that it is not so?'

[CEBES.] 'We have not.'

[SOCRATES.] 'What, then? If it is so, is not swift dissolution proper to the body, and, on the other hand, an indissolubility, complete, or something near to that, proper to the soul?'

[CEBES.] 'No doubt of it.'

[SOCRATES.] 'Reflect,' he said. 'When the man is dead, the visible part of him, the body, and the part that lies in the realm of what is seen, the thing we call a corpse, whose lot it is to be dissolved, to fall apart, and to be blown away, does not immediately suffer any of these things, but continues as it is for a reasonable length of time. Yes, if one ends with the body in good shape, it remains in some such youthful bloom as well as for a good long while. In fact, a body that has been collapsed and been embalmed, as the mummies lie embalmed in Egypt, will remain almost entire for an incalculable time. Even when the body rots, there are some parts of it, as bones and sinews, all that sort of thing, that nevertheless are, so to speak, immortal. Is n't it so?'

[CEBES.] 'Yes.'

[SOCRATES.] 'On the other hand, the soul, then, that which is invisible, which departs into a place elsewhere of like description, a region noble, pure, unseen, into the realm of *Hades* [the *invisible*] as it is truly called, to the God who is good and wise, whither, please God, my own soul too must shortly go; is she, I ask—this soul of ours which is like that, and is so formed by nature—is she, the moment she is separated from the body, to be dispersed and perish, as the majority of men declare? Far from it, my dear Simmias and Cebes! No, far rather what occurs is this.

'If the soul is pure when she departs, drawing with her nothing of the body, since in life she did not willingly in any manner hold communion with it, but fled from it, and drew herself together in herself, this being always her concern—and that means nothing else than rightly loving wisdom [rightly studying philosophy], and practising the act of death without complaining; would that, or would it not, be cultivating death?'

81

[CEBES.] 'By all means yes.'

[SOCRATES.] 'So, if she is in this condition, she goes away to what is like her, the invisible, to the divine, immortal, wise, where on her arrival she attains a state of happiness, released from error, madness, fears, and brutal loves, and all the rest of human ills. There verily she dwells, as it is said of the initiated [in the Mysteries], for the time remaining, with the gods. Shall we state it, Cebes, thus, or otherwise?'

[CEBES.] 'Thus, by Heaven!' answered Cebes.

[SOCRATES.] 'But methinks if when she is divided from the body she is sullied and uncleansed, because ever she consorted with the body, and tended it and loved it; and was bewitched by it and its desires and pleasures, so that she thought there was no other truth save bodily, what one could touch and see, drink, eat, and use for carnal love; whereas what for the eyes is shadowy and unseen, but can be known [is noumenal] and can be seized on by philosophy, this she was wont to hate, and tremble at, and flee; do you fancy that a soul in this condition when severed from the body can be herself, and by herself, without alloy?'

[CEBES.] 'Never in the world,' he said.

[SOCRATES.] 'Nay rather, I imagine, she would be shot through with the corporeal, which her familiarity and association with the body have implanted in her through her constant presence with it and her great concern for it?'

[CEBES.] 'Yes, certainly.'

[SOCRATES.] 'But this corporeal element, my friend, we are bound to think, bears downward, is heavy, earthy, visible. And therewith laden, a soul like that sinks down and is drawn back into the visible realm by fear of the invisible and of Hades [the unseen] as it is called; to haunt the neighborhood of tombs and sepulchres, about which the shadowy phantoms of souls have actually been seen, such images as are produced by souls like that, which were not released in purity, but participate in the visible; that is just why we can see them!'

[CEBES.] 'It seems likely, Socrates.'

[SOCRATES.] 'I should say so, Cebes! And what is more, they are not the souls of the good; no, they are the souls of the bad that are forced to wander in such places, paying for their former evil way of life. And they wander till the craving of the bodily element which keeps company with them once more imprisons them in a body. As is natural, they are imprisoned in creatures of like disposition to what they themselves cared for in life.'

[CEBES.] 'What sort of dispositions, Socrates, have you in mind?'

[SOCRATES.] 'I mean, for instance, that the ones who gave themselves to gluttony, to insolence, and to drink, and took no care to shun it, would be likely to put on the shape of asses and animals like that. Do n't you think so?' 82

[CEBES.] 'What you say is altogether probable.'

[SOCRATES.] 'Those who had a preference for injustice, tyranny, and robbing would put on the shape of wolves and hawks and vultures. Or should we say that souls like these would have some other destination?'

[CEBES.] 'Of course,' said Cebes, 'they would enter shapes like that.'

[SOCRATES.] 'Then evidently,' said he, 'in all the other cases the individual class would take its way according to resemblances, according to the thing its interest resembled?'

[CEBES.] 'That is evident,' he said; 'it must be so.'

[SOCRATES.] 'Even among these,' he said, 'the happiest, and they who go into the best locality, are they not the ones who practised the civic and communal virtue which is conjointly called temperance and justice, and is born of habit and activity, without philosophy and reason?'

[CEBES.] 'In what way, now, are these the happiest?'

[SOCRATES.] 'In this, that they are likely to pass back again into a comparable species, civilized and orderly, bees, let us say, or wasps, or ants, or even back into their actual human kind, and so there will be born from them good men.'

[CEBES.] 'That is likely.'

[SOCRATES.] 'As for the company of gods, to no one is it granted to attain to that save him who has pursued philosophy, and departed hence entirely pure—no, only to the one who is in love with learning.

'So there you have the reason, my dear Simmias, you and Cebes, why the true philosophers hold back from all the bodily desires, resist them, and will not give up to them; nor fear the loss of wealth, or poverty, as do the money-loving crowd; nor yet are they afraid of lack of honor, and of glory, from a low estate, as are they who wish for power and dignity. And so they hold aloof from those desires.'

[CEBES.] 'To yield would not become them, Socrates,' said Cebes.

[SOCRATES.] 'No, by Heaven! it would not,' said he. 'And therefore, Cebes, he says good-by to the others one and all, he who has a care for his own soul, and does not spend his life in pampering his body. He does not follow the same path as those who know not whither they are going. Himself convinced that one must not run counter to philosophy and her deliverance and cleansing, he turns to her, and follows where she leads.'

[CEBES.] 'How, Socrates?'

[SOCRATES.] 'I will tell you,' he replied. 'They who love learning are aware,' said he, 'that the soul when she was taken over by philosophy [for treatment] was completely fettered in the body, simply glued to it, and, instead of viewing things alone and by herself, forced rather to inspect them through the body as from a dungeon, and weltering in total ignorance. And philosophy perceived the ingenuity of the dungeon as being the production of desire, so that the prisoner himself might well be chief collaborator in his own imprisonment. And so I say, lovers of learning are aware that, once philosophy has received their soul in this condi-

83

tion, it gently reassures her, and endeavors to release her; showing her that observation with the eyes is full of fallacy, fallacious with the ears too and the other senses; persuading her to withdraw from these so far as she is not compelled to use them; urging her to gather and rally herself into herself, to put her faith in nothing but herself alone whenever she will for herself know, in and for itself, some true reality; whereas whenever she inspects through other instruments a thing that changes under changed conditions, she will think it nothing true because that sort of thing is sensible and visible, but what she sees herself is noumenal and invisible as well.

'Accordingly, the soul of the true philosopher believes that she ought not to struggle against this release, and so, as far as she is able, holds aloof from pleasures and desires, and from pain and fear. She reasons that when anybody is intensely pleased, or pained, or frightened, or given to desire, the evil he then suffers is (among the evils that one might imagine) of no such [minor] magnitude as falling sick or losing money because of one's desires; no, what he suffers is the greatest of all evils and the utmost, and yet he does not take account of it.'

[CEBES.] 'What is this evil, Socrates?' said Cebes.

[SOCRATES.] 'That every human soul when it is pleased or pained excessively is at the same time forced to take the source of this experience to be the very pinnacle of clarity and truth, although it is not so; for the sources are, above all else, objects that are visible. Is n't it so?'

[CEBES.] 'Yes, certainly.'

[SOCRATES.] 'And in this experience, above all, is the soul not fettered by the body?'

[CEBES.] 'How?'

[SOCRATES.] 'In that every pleasure, every pain, as with a rivet nails her to the body, pins her there, and renders her corporeal, causing her to take for true those things which the body happens to aver. From judging as the body does, and delighting in the same things it delights in, she is forced, methinks, to grow like it in character and culture, and so never can reach Hades in a state of purity, but must always make her exit full of bodily contamination. The result is that she quickly falls into another body, and, as if sown, is there implanted, and consequently has no lot in the association with that which is divine and pure and changeless.'

[CEBES.] 'Your statements, Socrates,' said Cebes, 'are absolutely true.'

[SOCRATES.] 'There you have the reasons, Cebes, why they who in the right sense are in love with learning are temperate and brave; and it is not upon the grounds which the multitude allege. Or do you think it is?'

[CEBES.] 'Not I, in any case.'

84 [SOCRATES.] 'No, indeed. On the contrary, the soul of a philosopher would argue thus, and would not think that, while it was the function of philosophy to release her, yet, once she was in process of release, she ought to give herself again to pleasures and pains, and tie herself once more, endlessly performing a labor like Penelope's reversed, raveling and reweaving the web.[8] No, she brings a calm of the emotions, follows reason, and abides in it, contemplating what is true, divine, and independent of opinion, and nourished by it; thus she thinks she ought to live while life shall last, and when life ends, she thinks that she will come to what is of one nature with her and is such as she, and so will be relieved of human ills. Thus nourished, and with aims like these, there is no terror for her, Simmias and Cebes; never fear that when she is severed from the body, she will be rent to pieces, dissipated by the winds, and carried off, to have no being anywhere for evermore.'

[PHAEDO.] When Socrates had spoken thus, there was silence for a long while. Socrates himself, to look at him, remained absorbed in the foregoing argument, and so were most of us. Cebes, though, and Simmias were arguing quietly together, and when Socrates saw that, he asked the two:

[SOCRATES.] 'How now?' said he. 'To you, perhaps, what has been said does not appear to be enough? It does, indeed, leave room for various misgivings, and is open to attack at several points, certainly if one is going to work the matter out with due precision.

[8] What Penelope wove by day she raveled by night.

If what you are considering is something else, I have not a word to say; but if you are in trouble over these misgivings, have no hesitation. Speak out, and go through any argument that you clearly think to be superior, and take me too along with you as helper, if you think you will make any better progress in my company.'

[SIMMIAS.] And Simmias replied: 'Yes, Socrates, I will tell you truly. The fact is that for some time now in our perplexity each of us has egged the other on, and urged him to inquire of you; we are eager to listen, but held back for fear of making trouble that you would not relish on account of the calamity impending.'

[SOCRATES.] On hearing that, he gave a quiet laugh, and said: 'Ah, Simmias! I fancy I might have hard work convincing other people that I do not think my present situation a calamity, when I cannot get even you men to believe me, but instead you fear that I am feeling sadder at the moment than I felt throughout my life before. And it looks as if you thought me inferior, in the art of divination, to the swans; for they, having chanted hitherto as well, yet when they feel that the time has come for them to die, now more than ever 85 chant with all their might, rejoicing that they are about to go away into the presence of the god whose ministers they are. But men, because of their own fear of death, malign the swans too, saying that they bewail their death, and sing their exit-song for grief; without reflecting that no bird sings when it is hungry, cold, or suffering in any way whatever; no, not the very nightingale, swallow, and hoopoe, the birds that, by tradition, when they sing lament for grief. To me it clearly is not so; neither these, nor yet the swans, lament when they are chanting; rather, methinks, they sing because, as servants of Apollo, they are inspired, and sing foreseeing the good things in Hades, and on that day exult far more than ever they did in the time preceding. I, too, believe myself to be a fellow servant of the swans, and consecrated to the same divinity, and think that I am not inferior to them in the power of divination which I have from our Master, and that I am no more despondent than are they in taking leave of life. No indeed, so far as that goes you must say and ask whatever you wish while the Council of Eleven for the City let you do it.'

[SIMMIAS.] 'That is excellent,' said he; 'and so, for my part, I will tell you what my trouble is, and Cebes here, in turn, will say wherein he is unable to accept what has been said. The fact is, Socrates, that in questions such as these, it seems to me, as no doubt it does to you, it is, if not impossible, yet a matter of the utmost difficulty to have certain knowledge in this present life; while, on the other hand, not to test in every way what people say of them, and to give up the search before one is worn out in studying them from every side, I take to be the part of a quite spineless fellow. Indeed you have to deal with them in one of these [three] ways: either get taught at every opportunity, or find out for yourself, or else, if these alternatives are impossible, then take what is at all events the best and most impeccable among the traditions of mankind, and let yourself be ferried [like Odysseus] upon that as on a raft, whereon to risk making the voyage through life, if you cannot travel through more safely and with smaller risk by a firmer means of transport—namely, some doctrine from above. So, further, I have now for my part no reluctance about asking you, since that is just what you are telling me to do, nor shall I in time to come have reason to accuse myself because I did not now say what I thought; for, Socrates, now that I and Cebes have both of us examined what was said, it does not seem to me to have been adequate at all.'

[SOCRATES.] And Socrates replied: 'It is quite probable, my friend, that you are right in thinking so. But say precisely where it is inadequate.'

[SIMMIAS.] 'It is so, to me,' said he, 'in this way; in that one might use this very argument with regard to harmony and a lyre together with its strings. The harmony is a thing invisible, and incorporeal, very beautiful and divine, present in the lyre that has been tuned; the lyre itself and its strings are bodies, are corporeal, synthetic, of the earth, and akin to what is mortal. Well, let someone smash the lyre, and cut and tear the strings to pieces; could anybody forcibly maintain, with reasoning the same as yours, that of necessity the harmony in question must still exist, and could not possibly have been destroyed? Could he hold it inconceivable that the lyre with its strings all broken, and the strings, which are of mortal nature, should remain, but that the harmony, which is of one nature and one kin with the divine and the immortal, should be destroyed, and destroyed before the mortal? Would he ever hold that, of necessity, the harmony by itself must somewhere still exist, and that the wood and strings will rot away before anything happens to it? Surely, though, Socrates, you must yourself, I do believe, have entertained the notion which we [of our school] specially uphold, that the soul is something of this order; that our body being strung as it were, and held together by the hot and the cold, the dry and the moist, and elements like those, our soul is a fusion and harmony of these elements when they are duly mixed and in proportion to each other. If the soul, then, really is a harmony, why, manifestly, when our body is relaxed unduly, or unduly stretched, by sickness or by harm of other sorts, the soul perforce must straightway be destroyed even though she is in the highest measure divine, like every other harmony in notes and in all the works of the masters; whereas what is left of individual bodies long persists, until either it is burnt or it rots away. See therefore what we are to say against this argument, if any one contends that, since the soul is a fusion of the elements in the body, in what is known as death she will perish first.'

[SOCRATES.] Then Socrates, as he was often wont to do, gave a broad stare, and, smiling, said: 'Indeed, what Simmias says is right enough. And so, if any one of you is readier than I am, why not reply to him? He would seem, in fact, to have dealt by no means weakly with the argument. And yet, before answering him, I think that we ought first to hear from Cebes, and learn what he in turn objects to in the argument. The interval will give us time to plan what we shall say. Thereafter, having heard them both, either we shall yield to them, if we think they are at all in tune, or, if they are not, then, and not till then, we shall uphold the argument. Come on now, Cebes,' he said, 'and tell us what it was that has upset you.'

[CEBES.] 'Well then, I will tell you,' answered Cebes. 'To me, the argument clearly stands just where it was, and is open to the same objection that we raised in the preceding stages. That our soul

existed also before entering this human shape I do not deny; with
that I am quite content, and, if you will let me say so, it has been
quite amply proved. But that when we are dead it anywhere continues to exist, I do not think has been so proved. That the soul is
not a thing more stable and enduring than the body, there I do not
yield to Simmias' objection, for in all these ways, 'it seems to me,
the soul is far superior. "Then why," the argument might say,
"are you still unconvinced, since you see, when the man is dead,
the frailer part of him persisting? Do you not think that necessarily
the more enduring part will be preserved over this length of time?"
Consider now if my reply to that has any force; for naturally I
too have need, like Simmias, of an image. With equal justice you
might speak of an old weaver who had died, and use this argument:
"The weaver is not dead, but is somewhere safe and sound." [In
the image or analogy, the 'weaver' stands for the soul, and his
'garment' for the body.] And as evidence you would offer the
mantle that he wore (which he himself had woven), because it
was preserved, and had not been destroyed. And if any one did not
believe you, you would ask: "Which kind of thing is more enduring, the man or the garment that is used and carried?" Whereupon
if some one answered that in kind the man is far more lasting,
you would fancy you had proved that, above all, the man is safe
and sound, because the less enduring part is not destroyed!

'But, Simmias, that, methinks, is not the way the matter stands.
And do you too consider what I said; for all can see that any one
who talks like that is talking nonsense. The fact is that our weaver
having worn out many garments of the sort, and woven them, he
perished after all those many, though, methinks, before the last
one, yet this last gives no more warrant for arguing that a man is
something worse and frailer than a garment. But, methinks, this
selfsame image may be accepted for the soul in its relation to the
body, and any one who said just that about them would, to my
mind clearly speak aright—that the soul is lasting, the body frailer
and not so enduring. But in fact, he would maintain, each several
soul wears out many bodies, certainly when any one lives many
years; the supposition is that while the man remains alive, the

body, being in a state of flux, keeps perishing, whereas the soul goes on weaving ever anew the tissue that is worn away. Of necessity, however, the soul, when her time came to perish, would have the garment which she happened to have woven last, and would perish in advance of this one only. But once let the soul be destroyed, and without delay the body would show its natural weakness, and, quickly rotten, disappear. And so we have no right to trust this argument for any hope that after we are dead our soul goes on existing anywhere.

'For suppose you granted to the man who argued thus even more 88 than we did grant. Concede to him not only that our souls existed before we were born, but that also after we are dead there is nothing to prevent the souls of some from still existing, and going on into the future, and being born repeatedly and thereafter dying; the assumption being that the thing by nature is so hardy that the soul can endure repeated birth. But when all that is conceded, your opponent will grant nothing further; he will not concede that she has not suffered in her many births, or that, having reached her end in some one death, she may not absolutely perish. This death, however, and this dissolution of the body, which brings destruction to the soul, is a thing, our disputant would say, that nobody knows about, for none of us can have any experience of it whatsoever. If that is so, then no one has a right to feel assured concerning death, nor is assurance warranted by good sense, unless one has a means of proving that the soul is something absolutely indestructible and immortal. Otherwise, a man who is about to die must always necessarily be in fear about his soul, afraid that in the moment when her union with the body is disrupted she will be utterly destroyed.'

[PHAEDO.] Well, after we had heard them, we all felt ill at ease, as later we confessed to one another; because we had been thoroughly convinced by the argument preceding theirs, and now we thought they had once more upset us, and plunged us into disbelief, an incredulity not only with respect to the arguments that went before, but also towards any that were going to be offered later. We feared that we might be unfit to judge of anything, or even that the matter in itself would not be capable of proof.

ECHECRATES. By Heaven! Phaedo, I forgive you if you did. Why, actually, just from listening to you now, I was on the point of saying something like that to myself: 'Then what argument are we ever going to trust, when the reasoning of Socrates, which was so utterly persuasive, has fallen now into discredit?' Now as ever, this doctrine that our soul is a kind of harmony has for me a wonderful fascination. And the recital of it has, so to speak, reminded me that hitherto this was my own opinion, and once more I direly need some other line of argument, from the outset as it were, to convince me that when we die the soul does not die with us. So tell us, in the name of Heaven! How did Socrates pursue the argument? And did he too show himself to be at all depressed, as you say you others were? Or, on the contrary, did he calmly go to the rescue of the argument? And were his efforts adequate or wanting? Tell us every bit of it as exactly as you can.

PHAEDO. In truth, Echecrates, I have often been amazed at Socrates, but never did I feel more admiration for him than on that occasion there beside him. That such a man as he should be able to reply was perhaps not unexpected. But, for my part, what I marveled at above all else in him was, first, the charm, good will, and approbation with which he took the issue the young men had raised; next, how keenly he perceived the painful effect their arguments had produced in us; and lastly, with what skill he healed us, and, as it were, when we had fled and were defeated, recalled and turned us to accompany him and join with him in testing out the argument.

ECHECRATES. How did he?

PHAEDO. I will tell you. I happened to be sitting at his right, beside the couch, upon a stool, so that he was a good deal up above me. So he began to stroke my head, and to clasp the locks of hair upon my neck, for on occasion he was in the habit of playing with my hair.

[SOCRATES.] 'Well,' said he, 'to-morrow, Phaedo, I suppose you will have these lovely locks cut off?'

[PHAEDO.] 'It would seem so, Socrates,' said I.

[SOCRATES.] 'Not if you will be advised by me.'

[PHAEDO.] 'What then?' said I.

[SOCRATES.] 'It is to-day,' said he, 'that I must cut mine too, and you cut yours, if actually this argument of ours is done for, and we cannot bring it back to life. As for me, if I were you, and the argument got away from me, I would, like the Argives, take an oath not to wear my hair till I renewed the fight, and won against the argument of Simmias and Cebes.'

[PHAEDO.] 'But,' said I, 'with two, as the story goes, not even Heracles could cope.'

[SOCRATES.] 'Then summon me,' said he, 'to be your Iolaus, as long as there is light.'

[PHAEDO.] 'Well then, so I do,' said I, 'but not as Heracles; instead, as Iolaus calling out for him.'

[SOCRATES.] 'It will make no difference,' he said. 'But first of all we must take care not to suffer a sad mischance.'

[PHAEDO.] 'How so?' said I.

[SOCRATES.] 'We must not come,' said he, 'to be *misologists* [haters of discourse], like people who grow into *misanthropes* [haters of mankind]; it is impossible,' said he, 'for any one to suffer any evil worse than this of hating argument. But *misology* and *misanthropy* issue from the same condition; for *misanthropy* comes from trusting some one beyond measure without knowledge of him, and thinking that the man is altogether true, and sound, and faithful, and then a little later finding him to be a wicked man and faithless; and similarly with the next man. And when any one has had this happen to him often, and endured it above all from those he took to be his most familiar friends and comrades, after frequent disillusionment he ends by hating every one, and thinking there is nothing sound in anybody anywhere. Have you never hitherto observed this process?'

[PHAEDO.] 'Indeed I have,' said I.

[SOCRATES.] 'Well,' said he, 'then isn't it disgraceful? And obviously such a person is attempting to deal with men while wanting skill in the knowledge of mankind? Surely, if he dealt knowingly

with the object as it really is, then he would judge that, on either
90 side, the very good and the very bad were few, while the great majority lay between.'

[PHAEDO.] 'How do you mean?' said I.

[SOCRATES.] 'Just as with respect,' said he, 'to what is very small and
very large. Don't you think it is rather seldom that we come upon
the very large or very small in man or dog or anything else you
like? Or the extreme, again, of swift or slow, of the ugly or the
beautiful, or of black or white? Or have you not observed in all
such cases that the extremes on either side are rare and few, while
the intermediates are plentiful and common?'

[PHAEDO.] 'Indeed I have,' said I.

[SOCRATES.] 'Well, don't you think that if a contest were set up for
wickedness, there too the eminent winners would be very few?'

[PHAEDO.] 'Quite likely,' I replied.

[SOCRATES.] 'Yes indeed,' said he. 'That, however, is not the point
of the comparison between arguments and men; but you led off in
a digression, and I followed. No, the point is this. Some one will
believe an argument to be correct, although he is unskilled in the
domain of arguments, and then a little later he will think it false,
as indeed it sometimes is, and again sometimes is not, and similarly with a second argument, and a third. And so, above all, as
you are well aware, they who spend their time in arguing pro and
con, on either side, finally believe that they have reached the highest stage of wisdom, and that they, they only, know that, alike in
things and arguments, there is nothing either sound or solid whatsoever. No, they think that all reality is in an ebb and flow just
like the changeful current in Euripus, never staying steady for a
moment.'

[PHAEDO.] 'You are absolutely right,' said I.

[SOCRATES.] 'So, Phaedo, it would be a pitiful mischance,' said he,
'when there really is an argument that is true and solid, and capable
of being grasped, if anybody then, because he has been present at
such arguments as, while still the same, appear at one time to be
true and at another false, should fail to blame himself and his own
lack of skill; if, instead, because of his pain he gladly shifted the

blame from his own shoulders and laid it on discourse; and if.from now on he should spend the rest of his life in hating and reviling arguments, and so should be deprived of the truth and the science of reality.'

[PHAEDO.] 'By Heaven,' I said, 'it would indeed be pitiful!'

[SOCRATES.] 'So there,' said he, 'is the first thing we must guard against, and we must not let the notion into the soul that perhaps there is nothing wholesome in discourse; far rather let us entertain the thought that we ourselves are not yet in sound condition, but must be valiant men and eager to attain that state, you and all the others for the sake of life, for all your life yet to come, I for death 91 alone; since at present, when this, death, is my main consideration, I run the risk of not behaving in true philosophic fashion, but, like those who are quite devoid of culture, of wishing to win! Look at them when they debate a question. Where the truth is in the subject of discussion they do not care; all they aim at is that their own propositions shall be accepted by the company attending. And therein, as I see it, lies all the difference, in the present case, between those persons and myself; for my aim is not to make those present think that what I say is true, save incidentally, but to convince myself as far as possible that it is so. This is the way I work it out, dear friend—and see how much I gain! If what I say is really so, how fine to have been convinced of it! But if there is nothing for us after we are gone, then at all events in this interval preceding death I shall not have worn the company out with lamentations. Meanwhile this uncertainty of mine will not last very long—that would indeed be bad!—but will be over in a little while. With this preliminary, Simmias and Cebes,' said he, 'I now come to the discussion. As for you, let me advise you to care little about Socrates, far more about the truth; if you think I utter truth, agree with me; if not, assail my argument at every point. Watch out that in my eagerness I do not, with my self-deceit, deceive you also, and, like a honey-bee, go off and leave my sting implanted in you!

'Come, we must march,' said he. 'First of all, remind me as to what you said, if you see that I do not remember. Simmias, I think, was doubtful and afraid that the soul, though both more divine and beautiful than the body, would be destroyed before it, as being on the order of a harmony. As for Cebes, he seemed to me to be in agreement with me upon this, that the soul at all events was more enduring than the body, but he did not think it clear to every one that after she had successively outlasted many bodies, the soul would not, on leaving her last body, at length now be herself destroyed; in which case, death is just this thing, the destruction of the soul, since, we know, the destruction of the body never ceases. Are not these the very matters, Simmias and Cebes, which we must investigate?'

[PHAEDO.] They both admitted it.

[SOCRATES.] 'Well, as to my previous arguments,' said he, 'do you reject them all, or only some of them, whereas others you do not?'

[SIMMIAS AND CEBES.] They both said: 'Some we do, and others we do not.'

[SOCRATES.] 'What do you say about the argument,' he asked, 'in which we held that learning is a reminiscence, and, if so, that necessarily our soul must have a previous existence elsewhere before it is imprisoned in the body?'

[CEBES.] 'For my part,' answered Cebes, 'at the time I was wonderfully taken with it, and now I stick to it as to no other argument.'

[SIMMIAS] 'That is my position, too,' said Simmias, 'and I should be very much astonished if, on this point anyway, I ever changed my mind.'

[SOCRATES.] And Socrates said: 'All the same, my Theban friend, you will have to change it, if you are going to keep this notion, that a harmony is something put together, and the soul a harmony combined from the bodily elements in tension; for surely you will not permit yourself to say that a harmony, a combination, was in existence before those elements from which it must be put together. Or will you?'

[SIMMIAS.] 'No, never, Socrates,' said he.

[SOCRATES.] 'Then do you see,' said he, 'that what you say amounts to this, when you state that the soul exists before she enters into human shape, into a body, and, on the other hand, that her existence is the combination of parts not yet in being? Your harmony, in fact, is not the sort of thing to which you liken it; no, the lyre, the strings, the sounds as yet unharmonized, come into being first, and last of all the harmony is formed, and it is first to perish. So how will this argument of yours chime with the one in question?'

[SIMMIAS.] 'In no way,' answered Simmias.

[SOCRATES.] 'And yet,' said he, 'if any argument ought properly to be in tune, it is one concerning harmony!'

[SIMMIAS.] 'It ought indeed!' said Simmias.

[SOCRATES.] 'So this one,' he continued, 'is out of tune for you. Well, look; see which of the two statements you will choose, that learning is a reminiscence, or that the soul is a harmony.'

[SIMMIAS.] 'Oh, Socrates,' he said, 'I prefer the first by far! The other came to me without help of demonstration, by way of a certain similarity and fitness—the source from which most people get this view. I, for my part, am aware that arguments that make their point by means of similarities are impostors, and, unless you are on your guard against them, will quite readily deceive you, in geometry as in all else. But the argument about memory and learning rests upon a basis that is worthy of all acceptation; for it was laid down, in substance, that our soul, before entering a body, exists in such a state that her essence is an essence having the denomination, "true reality" ["that which is"]. This principle, I am convinced, I have fully and in my own right accepted. And so, upon these grounds, I must perforce reject the statement, whether from myself or from another, that the soul is a harmony.'

[SOCRATES.] 'But, Simmias, what of this?' said he. 'Do you think it natural for a harmony, or any other synthesis, to behave in a different way from the elements out of which it is composed?'

[SIMMIAS.] 'Not at all.'

93

[SOCRATES.] 'Nor, as I believe, would it either act on anything, or be acted on by anything, in a different way from that in which those elements would act or be acted on?'

[PHAEDO.] He agreed.

[SOCRATES.] 'Well then, is it not the nature of a harmony, not to go before the elements out of which it is composed, but to follow after them?'

[PHAEDO.] He shared this view.

[SOCRATES.] 'So a harmony cannot possibly have any movement, sound, or other quality, in opposition to its parts?'

[SIMMIAS.] 'Far from it,' he replied.

[SOCRATES.] 'But again, is not each individual harmony by nature what it is through the harmonizing of its elements?'

[SIMMIAS.] 'I do not understand,' said he.

[SOCRATES.] 'If they were further, and more fully, harmonized (supposing that the thing were possible!), would it not be more a harmony, and fuller, whereas if they were less, and not so fully, harmonized, would it not be less a harmony, and less complete?'

[SIMMIAS.] 'Yes, certainly.'

[SOCRATES.] 'Well then, does the same hold true of the soul, that, in the smallest elements, one soul is more a soul and in a larger measure than another soul, or is less, and in a smaller measure than another soul, this very thing, a soul?'

[SIMMIAS.] 'Never in the world,' said he.

[SOCRATES.] 'Look now, by Heaven!' said he. 'It is said of one soul that she has intelligence, and virtue, and is good, of another that she lacks intelligence, is possessed of wickedness, and is bad. Is it right to say so?'

[SIMMIAS.] 'It is indeed.'

[SOCRATES.] 'Then among those who take the soul to be a harmony, what will any of them make of these things in the soul, of virtue and of vice? Will he say that there are, in addition, another harmony, and a dissonance? And will he say that the one, the good soul, has been harmonized, and has in her, she being a harmony, a second harmony, but that the other soul is herself unharmonized, and also has in her no second harmony?'

[SIMMIAS.] 'For myself,' said Simmias, 'I can give no answer, but obviously that is pretty much what one would say who supported the view in question.'

[SOCRATES.] 'We did, however, previously agree,' said he, 'that one soul is not more a soul, nor less a soul, than any other; and this amounts to the admission that one harmony is not more a harmony, or more complete, nor less a harmony, or less complete, than any other. Is n't it so?'

[SIMMIAS.] 'Yes, certainly.'

[SOCRATES.] 'And that, in any case, the harmony, incapable of being more or less a harmony, can be neither more completely nor less completely harmonized. Is it so?'

[SIMMIAS.] 'It is.'

[SOCRATES.] 'But one that is incapable of being harmonized to a greater or a less extent, does it participate in harmony more fully or less fully, or in equal measure?'

[SIMMIAS.] 'In equal measure.'

[SOCRATES.] 'And so a soul, since one soul is not more or less this very thing, a soul, than is another soul, cannot be harmonized in the degree of either more or less?'

[SIMMIAS.] 'That is so.'

[SOCRATES.] 'But if that is her condition, then she cannot share more fully either in a lack of harmony or in harmony?'

[SIMMIAS.] 'She can not.'

[SOCRATES.] 'But again, if that is her condition, then can one soul share at all more fully than another in vice or virtue, if vice really is a want of harmony and virtue harmony?'

[SIMMIAS.] 'No more fully.'

[SOCRATES.] 'Yes, Simmias, but rather, I suppose, to keep the argu- 94 ment straight, no soul can share in vice, if indeed the soul is a harmony; for a harmony, since it is just that, and nothing else but harmony, surely never could participate in dissonance.'

[SIMMIAS.] 'No indeed!'

[SOCRATES.] 'Nor in that case, surely, could the soul, being simply soul and nothing else, participate in vice.'

[SIMMIAS.] 'How could she, from our premises?'

[SOCRATES.] 'From this argument should we not conclude that the souls of all living creatures alike will be good, if it be true that it is the nature of souls to be just that thing, namely souls?'

[SIMMIAS.] 'Yes, I think so, Socrates,' he said.

[SOCRATES.] 'And do you think that the statement is correct,' said he 'and that the argument would come to this result if the hypothesis were sound that soul is harmony?'

[SIMMIAS.] 'Never in the world,' he said.

[SOCRATES.] 'Now tell me this,' said he. 'Of all the elements in man, is it not the soul, and nothing else, that rules, especially when she is wise?'

[SIMMIAS.] 'I answer yes.'

[SOCRATES.] 'And do you say that she gives in to the conditions of the body, or actually runs counter to them? I mean, for instance, when one is hot and thirsty, does she draw one in the opposite direction, not to drink, and when one is hungry, not to eat? And there are innumerable other cases, no doubt, where we see the soul opposing the bodily demands. Is n't it so?'

[SIMMIAS.] 'Yes, absolutely.'

[SOCRATES.] 'Then again, did we not in our previous discussion agree that the soul, supposing her to be a harmony, never would give forth a sound contrary to the tension, the release, the plucking, and whatever else those elements underwent out of which she happened to be formed, but would follow after, and not lead on before them?'

[SIMMIAS.] 'Yes, we agreed on that,' he said. 'How could we avoid it?'

[SOCRATES.] 'How is it now? Does n't she now show herself to be doing just the opposite in every way, leading all those elements of which they say she is composed, and running counter to well-nigh every one of them throughout a lifetime, and in all ways acting as their master? Some she chastises more severely, and with pains, as in gymnastic art and medicine; others she more gently chastens, now with threats, and now with warnings, disputing with the passions, ires, and fears, as if to her they were an alien thing. The situation is much like that which Homer has depicted in the *Odyssey* where [20.17] he says of Odysseus:

> He smote his breast, and thus reproved his heart:
> "Endure, my heart; far worse hast thou endured!"

When he wrote that, do you think the poet had the notion of the soul as in herself a harmony? Did he fancy her of such a nature as to let herself be led by bodily conditions, and not rather to lead them and be their master—as a thing far more divine than any harmony?'

[SIMMIAS.] 'By Heaven, Socrates, to my mind you are right!'

[SOCRATES.] 'And so, my best of friends, for us it will not do at all to say that the soul is a harmony. If we did, it seems, we should be in disagreement not alone with Homer, bard divine, but ourselves in disagreement with ourselves.'

95

[SIMMIAS.] 'Precisely so,' said he.

[SOCRATES.] 'So far, so good,' said Socrates. 'Somehow, Harmonia, Theban goddess, has now, it would appear, grown tolerably benign to us. Then what of our affair with Cadmus, Cebes? How render him benign, and with what argument?'

[CEBES.] 'You, I take it, will discover one,' said Cebes. 'Certainly you handled this argument with reference to harmony in a fashion that amazed me, it was so unexpected. While Simmias argued on the point that troubled him, I thought it would be quite amazing if any one were to find a way of dealing with his objection. Accordingly, it seemed very strange indeed to me when his argument could not hold up for a moment under the first onslaught from yours. So I should not be astonished if the same thing happened to the argument of Cadmus!'

[SOCRATES.] 'Good friend,' said Socrates, 'no boasting! or the evil eye may make our argument that is about to be go all awry. Still, that rests with the Deity; whereas it is our business, in Homeric wise, to come in close, and make assay if there is any strength in your position. Now in sum and substance here is what you seek. You demand a demonstration that our soul is indestructible, immortal; for want of it, you think that a philosopher who is about to die in the assurance and conviction that when he is dead he will fare far better in the life beyond than if he finished his days in another life—you think that such a man is senseless and a fool in his sure conviction. But that the soul is clearly something durable and godlike, and that it was already in existence before we became men, do not, you hold, in any way prevent the following conclusions. All that, you say, points not to immortality, but indicates that the soul is very lasting, and could have existed in a previous state for an in-calculable length of time, and known and done a great variety of things; but that does not make her the least bit more immortal. Rather, the very entrance of the soul into a human body was the beginning of her ruin, say a disease; so that all her life here is a state of misery, and when she ends it in what is known as death, she is destroyed. You say that it makes no difference at all whether she comes into a body once, or does it many times, at all events so far as touches the individual person and his fear; he is bound to fear, if he has any sense, when he does not know, and has no argu-ment to offer that she is not mortal. That, I think, is just about what you are saying, Cebes. And I have purposely resumed it in detail, so that nothing may escape us, and that you may add or may with-draw whatever you see fit.'

[CEBES.]   And Cebes said: 'But indeed, at present there is nothing that I need, for my part, either to withdraw or to supply. Those are my actual views.'

[PHAEDO.]   Socrates now paused for a considerable time, absorbed in some reflection. Then:

[SOCRATES.]   'Your problem,' he said, 'is no light matter, Cebes, for it compels us thoroughly to examine the cause of generation and corruption as a whole. On the subject of these, if you desire, I will relate to you my own experience. Then, if anything in what I say appears to you to be of service, it will be for you to employ it in support of your position.'

[CEBES.]   'But indeed I do desire it,' replied Cebes.

[SOCRATES.]   'Then attend to my exposition. As a young man, Cebes,' he continued, 'I was wonderfully taken with that kind of learning which is known as Natural Science. To me it appeared sublime—to know the causes of each several thing, how everything comes to be, and is destroyed, and has existence! And frequently I was shifted back and forth, primarily with regard to questions like the follow-ing. Is it the case that when the hot and the cold fall into a sort of putrefaction, as some maintained, then living creatures are pro-duced? And what we think with, is it the blood, or is it the air, or fire? Or is it none of these, but it is the brain that yields the sensations of hearing, sight, and smell, and from these spring memory and judgment, while from memory and judgment, when they have got into a settled state, there arises, in this sequence, knowledge? And, conversely, I studied the corruption of these things, as also what the heavens and the earth go through; and the upshot was that, in my own opinion, I was by nature unfit beyond all comparison for this kind of research.

'Of that I will give you an adequate proof. Before, there had been matters which, as it seemed to me at all events and to all the rest, I fully understood, but now by this research I was so utterly blinded that I actually unlearnt those matters which heretofore I thought I knew; along with many other things, the reason, for example, why a man grows bigger. Heretofore I had thought that this was clear to every one—that the cause was eating and drinking: when food was taken, out of it flesh was added to flesh, and bone to bone, and by the selfsame process there thus was added to each several portion of the body what was proper to it; then that which was a little mass thereafter became large, and thus the little human being became big. So I then imagined. Does n't it look right to you?'

[CEBES.] 'To me, it does,' said Cebes.

[SOCRATES.] 'Now consider this as well. I took it I was warranted in thinking, when one saw a tall man standing beside a short, that he was taller precisely by his head, and that the same was true of horse compared with horse; or, for instances clearer yet than these, I thought, if ten were more than eight, it was because the two were added to the eight, and that the distance of two cubits was greater than of one because it exceeded the latter by one-half of its own length.'

[CEBES.] 'And what is your opinion now?' said Cebes.

[SOCRATES.] 'By Heaven!' he replied, 'I am pretty far from thinking that I know the cause of any of these things! For my part, I am not prepared to say, when you add one to one, whether the one to which you add one becomes two, or the added one and the one to which this one is added, through the addition of the second to the first, make two! I cannot comprehend why when they severally were apart from one another each of them was one, and the two

97

of them were not two, but when they approached each other, this, their mutual nearness, was the reason of their becoming two— the coming together caused by their approximation. No more can I persuade myself when unity is cut in two, that this, again, the separation, is the cause of there being two; for here the cause would be just the opposite of what it was before. Before, the reason was that the two items were brought close together, and the one was added to the other; but now the reason is that they are set apart, and separated from each other! As for what produces unity, I do not let myself believe I know that, either, nor, in a word, why any-thing else comes into being, is destroyed, or has existence. Not ac-cording to that method of investigation; no, I muddle along, with luck, by another method of my own; the method in question I do not accept at all.

'No, once I listened to some one reading from a book, by Anaxag-oras,' he said, 'where it was stated: Mind [*Nous*] it is, in fine, that orders all, and is of all things cause.[9] I took pleasure in this cause, and it seemed to me in a way quite right that Mind should be the universal cause; and I judged, if it were so, that the ordering Mind, in arranging all, would dispose each individual thing in the best conceivable way; and so, if anybody wished to find out how the individual thing arises, is destroyed, or has existence, he would have to find out this concerning it, namely, which is the best way for it to be, or undergo or do whatever it may do or suffer. Now from this line of reasoning, I thought, there was nothing else that it so much behoved a man to study, with regard both to the man him-self and to all other objects, as excellence and supreme perfection; but the said man must have, also, a knowledge of that which is worse; for the same knowledge is concerned with both. Consider-ing all this, I was rejoiced to think that I had found a teacher who could explain to me after my own mind the cause of all reality, Anaxagoras, who could tell me, first of all, if the earth is flat or round, and, when he told me, would inform me in detail why it is and must be so, referring to the better and the principle that it is better for the earth to be so shaped. And if he held that it was at

[9] Apparently not a direct quotation.

the centre, he would inform me in detail in what way it was better for the earth to be in that position. He would simply have to make the matter clear for me, and I was ready not to go on seeking for any other sort of cause. And with reference to the sun as well I was ready to receive the like instruction, and so for the moon and 98 all the stars, with regard to their comparative velocity, their tropic points, and all the rest of their phenomena; how far for each of these things it was better that they should do and undergo what they actually did and underwent. Never for a moment did I dream that, once he had asserted that these things were set in order by Mind, he would fetch in any other cause for them than that their best condition was for them to be precisely as they were. Assigning, then, to each of them, and to them all in common, the aforesaid cause, he would, I thought, explain in detail what was best for each, and what was the common good for all. And I would not have given up my hopes in exchange for a very large sum. No, but with what eagerness I seized upon the book, and read it as quickly as I could, so that as soon as possible I might know perfection and inferiority!

'From my wonderful dream, my friend, what a plunge I took, when, as I went on and read, I saw that the man had made no further use of Mind, and did not give it any place among the causes for the ordering of matters, but found causes in the air, the ether, and the water, and a lot of other curious things. What happened to him? In my opinion it was very much as if somebody were to say: "In all his actions, Socrates does everything with his mind," and then, in trying to explain the causes of each thing I do, began by saying that the reason why I am now sitting here is that my body is made up of bones and muscles, and that the bones are solid and have joints dividing them from one another, while the muscles, which can be contracted or relaxed, envelop the bones together with the flesh and the skin, which contains all the aforesaid parts; and so the swinging of the bones in their articulations, the release and the contraction of the muscles, make it possible for me, doubtless, now to flex my members; and there is the reason why I am sitting here drawn up in this position! And again, for this discussion with you, he could mention other causes of a similar sort, alleging vocal sounds, air, hearing, and innumerable other things; failing to mention what the actual reasons are—that, since the Athenians thought it better to condemn me, consequently I am here, and because, for my part, I thought it better to be seated here, more just to stay and undergo the penalty they have ordered. Whereas, by the Dog! I guess these bones and muscles would long since have been in the vicinity of Megara or Boeotia, carried thither by a concept of the Best, had I not thought that it would be more just and beautiful, instead of flight and escape, to accept at the hands of the City the penalty she set.

'But to label such things "causes" is simply too bizarre. If, however, anybody said that, wanting the possession of such things— bones, muscles, and whatever else belongs to me—I could not do what I intended, he would be right. But to say it is because of these that I do what I do, and that I do it with intelligence, but not by choosing what is best, would seem to be a very free and easy way of talking! It would mean that one could not distinguish what in reality was the cause from that for want of which the cause could never act. This last [the instrument] it is, to my mind, which most people, groping as in the dark, and using an improper term, clearly refer to as the cause. That is why one person, who has the earth surrounded by a vortex, thinks it is the heaven that keeps the earth in her place; whereas another likens her to a wide kneading-trough resting upon the air for her support. But the power by which the best arrangement there can be is the one in which these things at present are disposed, for that they do not seek; nor do they think that there is in it any force divine. No, they imagine that some day they are going to discover an Atlas stronger than ours, more undying, and more firmly sustaining all things. And they actually believe that the good, the fitting, binds and holds together nothing; but as for me, how gladly I would go to school to any one who could explain the working of a cause like that! But since I was deprived of it, and could neither find it by myself nor learn about it from another, I had to take the other tack in the quest after the cause. Would you like it, Cebes, if I gave you an account of that?' he asked.

[CEBES.] 'I should like it beyond measure!' he replied.

[SOCRATES.] 'Well then,' he continued, 'after that, once I had renounced the inquiry into being, I thought that I ought to guard against the mishap which comes to those who watch the sun in an eclipse while they observe it, for I understand they sometimes ruin their eyes because they do not look at its reflection in the water, or employ some similar device. So I had some such thing in mind, and was afraid I might become completely blind in the soul by gazing at things with my eyes and trying to apprehend them with each several sense. It seemed to me that I must take refuge in reasoning, and there inquire into the truth of things. It is possible, of course, that in a way my parallel is not exact, for I do not wholly grant that one who is investigating things in reasonings is looking at them in an image rather than in actuality. But at all events that is the way I went about it; so in each case taking as a basis the proposition which I judge to be most valid, then whatever I find to be in harmony with it I put down as true, whether it touches cause, or touches all else whatsoever. What is not in harmony with it, I put down as false. But I wish to make my meaning clearer to you, for I think that you do not at present understand it.'

[CEBES.] 'No, by Heaven!' answered Cebes. 'Not too well!'

[SOCRATES.] 'And yet,' said he, 'there is nothing at all new in what I say. Rather, it is what I have incessantly repeated, at all other times as in the argument now past; for herewith I shall attempt to show you the species of causality I worked out, and I go back to those well-known positions. From them I start, assuming that there is a beautiful in and for itself, and similarly a good, a great, and all the rest. If you grant me this, and agree that these exist, I hope to demonstrate to you thence, and thence to discover, the reason why the soul must be immortal.'

[CEBES.] 'But you may rest assured that I do grant you this,' said Cebes; 'so waste no time about getting on.'

[SOCRATES.] 'Then look,' said he, 'at what follows from those propositions, and see if here your views are in accord with mine; for it is clear to me that if anything is beautiful except the beautiful in itself, it is beautiful for no other reason than because it has a part in the said beautiful. And I say the same of all the rest. Is that the sort of cause which you agree to?'

[CEBES.] 'Yes,' he said, 'I agree to it.'

[SOCRATES.] 'And therefore,' he continued, 'I can get no further with those other causes, the learned ones; I can make no sense of them. No, if anybody tells me that an object, anything, is beautiful because it has a brilliant color, or a special shape, or any other quality like that, I say good-by to all of it, for all explanations trouble me save one. To this one I hold simply, artlessly, and perhaps in my simplicity, as mine, that nothing makes the object beautiful except the presence of the Beautiful aforesaid or partaking of it, by whatever way or means the addition of it comes about; for on this point up to now I make no confident assertion, and am only sure that by the Beautiful all beautiful things have beauty. There, it seems to me, is the safest answer I can give to myself or to another; and by holding to that I judge that I shall never stumble, but expect to be safe in giving answer to myself and anybody else that by the Beautiful beautiful things have beauty. Is n't that your view as well?'

[CEBES.] 'It is.'

[SOCRATES.] 'And similarly it is by Magnitude that the large things are large, and the larger are larger, and by Smallness that the less are less?'

[CEBES.] 'Yes.'

[SOCRATES.] 'And therefore you would not accept the statement if it were asserted that one man was taller than his fellow by a head, and the shorter was shorter than his fellow by a head. No, you would protest that, as for you, you make no other assertion than this: Every time one thing is greater than another, it is greater through no other thing than magnitude, and on that account is greater, on account of magnitude; and the smaller thing is smaller through no other thing than smallness, and on that account is smaller, on account of smallness. I take it you would be afraid of an objection if you stated that a man was greater by a head, and his fellow less. The opposing argument would, in the first place, urge that the greater was greater, and the less was less through the selfsame [head], and, secondly, that it was through the head, which is small, that the greater was greater, and that it would be monstrous if a man were large through something small. Or would n't you be afraid of that?'

[CEBES.]   And Cebes, laughing, said: 'I should, indeed!'

[SOCRATES.]   'Well,' said he, 'and would n't you be afraid to say that ten exceeded eight by two, and this was the cause of the excess, but not afraid to say that it was greater by a quantity and through quantity? And afraid to say that the distance of two cubits was greater than one cubit by one-half, but not that it was greater through magnitude? The fear, no doubt, would be the same?'

[CEBES.]   'Yes, certainly,' he said.

[SOCRATES.]   'But again. When one is added to one, would n't you be careful not to say that the addition was the cause for the production of the two? Or when unity is divided, that the division was the cause of it? "Never!" you would shout: "I do not know of any other way by which the individual object comes to be than by sharing in the proper essence of the particular reality in which it ought to share; and so in these two cases I have no other cause to offer for the appearance of the two except participation in duality; and so the things that are going to be two must share in this, as what is going to be one must share in unity." As for these divisions and additions, and all other like refinements, you would say good-by to them, and leave the problems to be answered by those men who are wiser than you!

'Meanwhile you, "in fear of your own shadow," as the saying goes, and of your inexperience, and clinging to the safe support of that basic proposition, would make answer in accordance with it. On the other hand, if anybody simply fastens on the premise, [neglecting the conclusions to be drawn from it], you would say good-by to him, and would give no answer till you looked into the consequences of that premise, to see if, in your opinion, they agree or disagree with one another. When, however, it comes time for you to give account of that premise itself, you must follow the same procedure, and supply another premise taken from those higher up [in the scale of universals], the one that clearly is most valid, and continue till you reach a principle that will hold. Meanwhile you must not get things mixed up, as the wrangling speakers do, and talk at once about the principle and the consequences that arise from it, at all events if you wish to find any real truth. About reality, of course, those people have not one thing to say, nor the least concern; they are so wise that they can make a mess of everything, and yet maintain their own self-satisfaction. As for you, if it is true that you are a philosopher, I think you will do as I say.'

102

[SIMMIAS AND CEBES.] 'What you say,' said Simmias and Cebes together, 'is absolutely true.'

ECHECRATES.   By Heaven, Phaedo, they were right enough! I think it is amazing how clear he made that explanation, even for a person of no great intelligence.

PHAEDO.   Yes indeed, Echecrates; and so it seemed to everybody who was there.

ECHECRATES.   And to us who were not, and are listening to it now. But tell us what was said after that.

PHAEDO.   As I think, the sequel went thus. When these concessions had been made to him, and it had been agreed that each individual idea had existence, and that things other than ideas got their names through their participation in the said ideas, after that he put this question:

[SOCRATES.] 'Now if that is what you hold to, then what of this? When you say that Simmias is larger than Socrates, but smaller than Phaedo, in that case do you say that both qualities are found in Simmias together, largeness and smallness alike?'

[CEBES.] 'Yes, I do.'

[SOCRATES.] 'But come,' said he; 'when you agree that "Simmias is larger than Socrates," is not the manner of expression to be distinguished from the actual truth? It is not that Simmias is by nature larger through his being Simmias; he is larger through his having such and such a magnitude. Nor is he larger because Socrates is Socrates, but through Socrates' having such and such a smallness in relation to the magnitude of Simmias.'

[CEBES.] 'True.'

[SOCRATES.] 'Nor, again, is he exceeded by Phaedo because Phaedo is Phaedo, but through Phaedo's having such a magnitude in relation to the smallness of Simmias.'

[CEBES.] 'That is so.'

[SOCRATES.] 'Thus Simmias comes to have the name of being small, and the name of being large, because he is between the two, and to the largeness of the one, to be exceeded by it, he submits his smallness, and to the other he presents his largeness, which exceeds the other's smallness.' And, with a smile, he said: 'I seem ready to declaim in prose; but it is, after all, very much as I say.'

[PHAEDO.] He assented.

[SOCRATES.] 'At all events, my reason for saying it is the wish that you shall share my views; for to me it is clear not only that essential magnitude never will let itself be at the same time great and small, but also that the magnitude present in us never will take on smallness, or allow itself to be exceeded. No, one of two things must take place. Either it must flee and be displaced when its opposite, the small, advances toward it, or when that approaches, it [magnitude] must cease to be; it refuses to hold its ground and, by admitting smallness, to be something different from what it was. Thus I, once I received and accepted smallness, and continuing to be the man I am, I, the said person, am small; whereas magnitude, being great, cannot endure to be small. And similarly the smallness that is in us will always refuse to become or to be great; nor will any other real thing, so long as it is what it is, at the same time let itself become or be its opposite. No, when this happens to it [when its opposite approaches], it either goes away or ceases to exist.'

103

[CEBES.] 'That seems absolutely right to me,' said Cebes.

PHAEDO. And one of the listening company (which one, I do not quite remember) said: 'Ye Gods! In your preceding argument, was not the very opposite admitted of what was said just now? Was it not agreed that the greater arises from the less, and the less from the greater, and, absolutely, that for opposites their genesis is just this, that they arise from opposites? But now, it seems to me, the statement is that the thing in question never can take place.'

And Socrates, turning his head toward the speaker, said:

[SOCRATES.] 'Gallant of you to remind us! But you fail to note the difference in our statements then and now. The statement then was that from an opposite thing the opposite thing is born. The statement now is that it is the opposite itself which never can pass into its own opposite, neither the opposite as it is found in us, nor as it is in its own [eternal] nature. At that time, friend, we spoke of things that have participation in the opposites, referring to them by the names of those realities; but now we speak of those realities by whose indwelling in the things, the things receive their names. Of the opposites themselves, we say that always they refuse to take their genesis from one another.' And at the same time turning to Cebes, he asked: 'Did not anything he said in any way disturb you, Cebes?'

[CEBES.] 'No,' said Cebes, 'I was n't troubled by it this time. That does not mean, however, that various doubts do not disturb me.'

[SOCRATES.] 'Well,' he said, 'are we in complete agreement as to this, that one opposite will never be the other?'

[CEBES.] 'Absolutely,' he replied.

[SOCRATES.] 'Then further, see,' said he, 'if we agree on this as well. There is something you term "hot," and something you term "cold"?'

[CEBES.] 'Yes.'

[SOCRATES.] 'Are they just what you call snow and fire?'

[CEBES.] 'By Heaven, no!'

[SOCRATES.] 'Then the hot is something else than fire, and the cold is something else than snow?'

[CEBES.] 'Yes.'

[SOCRATES.] 'But this, I take it, is your view, that snow, so long as it is snow, never will receive the hot in the way we previously described and still be what it was, snow, and, in addition, hot; no, when the hot approaches, the snow will either give way to it, or cease to be.'

[CEBES.] 'Yes, certainly.'

[SOCRATES.] 'And fire, again, when the cold approaches it, will either take itself away, or cease to be, but, once it has received the cold, never can permit itself to go on being what it was, fire, and, in addition, cold.'

[CEBES.] 'That is right,' he said.

[SOCRATES.] 'Then in certain cases like these,' he said, 'it is true not only that the form itself has a right to its own name for ever, but that there is something else, which is not the form in question, yet ever has the stamp thereof for the length of its existence. But here are other cases where, perhaps, my meaning will be clearer. The odd, no doubt, must always get this name which we now give to it. Is n't it so?'

[CEBES.] 'Yes, certainly.'

[SOCRATES.] 'Does this hold only of the real essence (that is my question), or is there something else as well, something which is not identical with the odd, which nevertheless must always carry 104 the same name as the reality because it is by nature such that it never can be separate from the odd? The sort of case I have in mind is that of the number three and many others. Consider what happens in the case of three. In your opinion, must it not always be described by its own name, and also by that of the odd, albeit this is not identical with three? But if that is natural to three, it will be so with five as well, and so with half the entire list of numbers, and thus, although no one of them is identical with the odd, each one is always odd. And, on the other hand, the number two, and four, and all the rest of the other series of numbers, while no one of them is identical with the even, yet every one of them is always even. Do you agree with that, or not?'

[CEBES.] 'How could I avoid it?' he replied.

[SOCRATES.] 'Now then,' said he, 'mark what I wish to bring out. It is this. Clearly it is not alone those primary opposites that will not admit each other; it is all those other things which, while not opposed to one another, yet always have the opposites within them, and which, apparently, will not receive the form opposed to the form that is within them, but at the approach of this are either destroyed or else displaced. Or shall we not assert that three will rather cease to be, will sooner undergo whatever else it can, than, while continuing to be three, to become even?'

[CEBES.]   'Most certainly,' said Cebes.

[SOCRATES.]   'But,' said he, 'there is n't any opposition between two and three.'

[CEBES.]   'No, there is n't.'

[SOCRATES.]   'So it is not the opposite forms alone which do not tolerate the approach of one another; no, there are certain other opposites that will not stand it.'

[CEBES.]   'You are absolutely right,' said he.

[SOCRATES.]   'Do you wish then, if we can,' said he, 'to have us settle what the nature of these is?'

[CEBES.]   'Yes, indeed.'

[SOCRATES.]   'Well then, Cebes,' he rejoined, 'they would be of such sort that when one of them has got possession of a thing, not only do they force it to contain their own idea, but also always to contain one that is opposite to another.'

[CEBES.]   'What do you mean?'

[SOCRATES.]   'What we just now said. You surely know that when things have become possessed by the idea of the three, they necessarily must be, not only three, but odd.'

[CEBES.]   'Yes, certainly.'

[SOCRATES.]   'But to such a thing, we hold, there never will come the idea opposite to that form which makes the thing.'

[CEBES.]   'No.'

[SOCRATES.]   'But the form that makes it is the odd?'

[CEBES.]   'Yes.'

[SOCRATES.]   'And the idea opposite to this is the form of even?'

[CEBES.]   'Yes.'

[SOCRATES.]   'Then to the three the idea of the even will never come.'

[CEBES.]   'Surely not.'

[SOCRATES.]   'The three has no part in the even?'

[CEBES.]   'It has none.'

[SOCRATES.]   'Then the triad is uneven.'

[CEBES.]   'Yes.'

[SOCRATES.]   'So there is what I said we should determine—what sort of things, while not opposed to any essence, will nevertheless not entertain its opposite; our example being now the triad, which, while it is not opposite to the even, will not a whit the more receive it, because the triad always carries with it the opposite idea to the even; just as the two carries with it the opposite to the odd, and fire the opposite to the cold, and similarly a host of other things. Well, see if you state matters thus: It is not the opposite idea only that will not receive its opposite; there is also the thing which carries with it an opposite idea to that toward which the thing proceeds; the carrier never will receive the opposite idea to the idea of what is carried. But go back, and think it over; repetition will do no harm. The five will not receive the idea of the even, nor the ten, which is twice five, that of the odd. The double is, meanwhile, in itself the opposite of something else, yet will not entertain the idea of the odd; the case is the same with three-halves, and other similar fractions having two in the denominator; they will not entertain the idea of the whole; so also with one-third and all the like—if you follow me indeed, and share in these positions.'

[CEBES.] 'I agree with all my heart,' said he, 'and follow you.'

[SOCRATES.] 'Go back,' said he. 'Begin at the beginning, and tell me what I ask, not echoing my words, but matching my procedure. I say so for this reason. In addition to the answer I then put first, that safe reply, I see another means of safety, to be drawn from what has just been said. Suppose you were to ask me what it is that must be present in the body to make the body warm; I would not give you the safe answer, that unlearned one, "It is the hot." No, I would give the more refined one from our position now: "It is fire." And if, again, you asked me what it is whose presence in the body makes it sick, I would not say, "Disease." No, my answer would be, "Fever." Nor if you asked what it is in a number that will make it odd, I do not say, "The odd," but "Unity"; and so with all the rest. But see if you now understand my meaning well enough.'

[CEBES.] 'I understand it very well indeed,' said he.

[SOCRATES.] 'Then answer this,' said he. 'What will it be that, in the body, makes it live?'

[CEBES.] 'It will be the soul,' said he.

[SOCRATES.] 'And is that always so?'

[CEBES.] 'How could any one,' he said, 'deny it?'

[SOCRATES.] 'Then whatever be the object upon which the soul lays hold, she invariably comes to it bringing life?'

[CEBES.] 'Yes, that is what she does,' said he.

[SOCRATES.] 'Is there anything opposed to life, or nothing?'

[CEBES.] 'Yes, there is.'

[SOCRATES.] 'What?'

[CEBES.] 'Death.'

[SOCRATES.] 'Then the soul cannot at any time receive the opposite of what she always brings with her, as must be admitted from our previous conclusions?'

[CEBES.] 'And admitted to the last degree!' said Cebes.

[SOCRATES.] 'And then? What will not entertain the idea of the even, how did we just now name it?'

[CEBES.] 'The uneven,' he replied.

[SOCRATES.] 'And that which will not entertain the just, and what will not receive the musical [artistic]?'

[CEBES.] 'Inartistic,' he replied, 'and for the other, the unjust.'

[SOCRATES.] 'Good! And what would never receive death, how do we call that?'

[CEBES.] 'Undying,' he replied.

[SOCRATES.] 'And the soul does not receive death?'

[CEBES.] 'No.'

[SOCRATES.] 'The soul, then, is a thing undying?'

[CEBES.] 'Is a thing undying.'

[SOCRATES.] 'Good!' said he. 'Shall we say that this has now been proved? Or how does it look to you?'

[CEBES.] 'Proved most amply, Socrates!'

[SOCRATES.] 'Then, Cebes,' said he, 'what follows? If by necessity the odd were indestructible, could three be otherwise than indestructible?'

[CEBES.] 'Certainly not.'

[SOCRATES.] 'Well, suppose that, by necessity, the non-hot could not be destroyed; whenever anybody put the hot to snow, the snow would take itself away, its essence safe and undissolved. It surely would not perish, nor, on the other hand, would it remain and receive the heat.'

[Cebes.] 'That is true,' he said.

[Socrates.] 'And the same thing would be true, I judge, if the non-coolable could not be destroyed. Whenever anything cold came at the fire, the fire would not go out, nor cease to be, but would be off in safety, and away.'

[Cebes.] 'Of necessity,' he said.

[Socrates.] 'And must one not say the same thing necessarily of the immortal? If the immortal too is indestructible, then for the soul it is impossible to perish when death comes at her; since, from the arguments preceding, it follows certainly that death she will not entertain, nor shall she be a spirit that has died; no more than three, as we have said, ever will be even, nor again, will odd be even, nor fire be cold, nor yet the heat that is in fire.

'Perhaps some one will say: "While, as we agreed, the uneven never becomes even at the approach of the even, yet what is there to keep it then from perishing, and the even from then coming into being in its place?" Against one who argued thus we could not contend that the uneven does not perish, since it is not indestructible; for if we were agreed on that, it would be easy for us to retort that on the approach of the even, the uneven and three retire and go away. And in similar wise we could retort with reference to fire, the hot, and all the rest, could we not?'

[Cebes.] 'We could indeed.'

[Socrates.] 'And so now with respect to the immortal. If we are agreed that it is also indestructible, then the soul would be, not immortal only, but indestructible as well. If we are not agreed, the case demands another argument.'

[Cebes.] 'But there is no need of one, at all events upon this question. What else conceivably would not receive destruction, if that which is immortal, and thus eternal, could receive it?'

[Socrates.] 'The Deity at least, I think,' said Socrates, 'and the form itself of life, and whatever else may be immortal, by general consent would be allowed to be for ever indestructible.'

[Cebes.] 'Heavens, yes!' said he. 'By general consent of men—nay more, I think, of gods as well.'

[Socrates.] 'When now what is immortal is also indestructible, must not the soul, if she is found to be immortal, be indestructible as well?'

[CEBES.] 'By absolute necessity!'

[SOCRATES.] 'Accordingly, when death comes to a man, it is the mortal part of him, so it would seem, that dies, while the immortal, safe and indestructible, retires and goes away, giving place to death.'

[CEBES.] 'That is clear.'

[SOCRATES.] 'Above all else, then, Cebes,' said he, 'soul is immortal and indestructible; and in very truth our souls will dwell in Hades.'

[CEBES.] 'For my part, Socrates,' said he, 'I have nothing else to add, and am in no way doubtful of the arguments presented. But if Simmias here, or anybody else, has anything to offer, it would be well for him to have his say. If there is anything he wants to urge or hear about such questions, I do not see how any one who puts it off will get another opportunity.'

[SIMMIAS.] 'No,' said Simmias. 'I, for my part, have no further doubt on any point, at all events so far as touches the arguments presented. And yet the magnitude of what we are discussing, and my poor opinion of humanity in its weakness, force me, inwardly, to be distrustful still of the conclusions.'

[SOCRATES.] 'Your statement, Simmias,' said Socrates, 'does not apply to them alone; you are quite right about our premises as well. And sound as these may seem to you, they nevertheless deserve a closer scrutiny. And once you have adequately sifted them, I think you will follow out the argument as far as it is possible for any man to go. If you make sure that you have done so, you need seek no further.'

[SIMMIAS.] 'You are right,' said he.

[SOCRATES.] 'But here, Gentlemen,' said he, 'is something that you would do well to think about. If the soul is really immortal, she needs care not only for this length of time which we call "life," but for all time. And in this present it would seem to be a dreadful risk to take, should any one neglect her. If death were a release from everything, what a godsend it would be for bad men, when they die, to be freed at once from the body, and, together with the soul, from their own wickedness! As it is, since she is seen to be immortal, there is no other refuge for her from her ills, no other safety, except becoming just as good and wise as she can be. The soul comes into Hades bringing nothing with her but her discipline and her way of life. And these, tradition has it, are what most aid or injure the deceased from the very outset of the journey yonder.

'Here is the tradition. When a person dies, the genius [*daimon*] that each individual has by lot while he is living seeks to lead him to a certain place, the place where the dead are brought together to be judged, and whence they journey on to Hades in company with their guides, whose office it is to attend those journeying from this world to the next. But when they have there endured the lot that falls to them, and have remained for the time they must, another guide conveys them back again, in the course of many and protracted cycles. So the journey is not as the Telephus of Aeschylus describes it, for he says that simple is the way that leads to Hades! To me it clearly is not simple, no, nor single; were it, there would be no need of guides, for nobody, I guess, would miss the road if there were only one. But in fact there seem to be many forks and cross-roads, as I judge from the evidence of rites and usages with us. Then the soul that is orderly and prudent follows willingly, and does not feel lost in her surroundings. But the soul that is enamoured of the body, she, as I said before, for a long time lingers fluttering round the body and the realm of sight, and hardly, after many struggles and much anguish, is she forcibly led on her way by the genius thereto appointed. And now she comes unto the place where are the other souls. And if she is uncleansed of an evil she has done, is guilty of such crimes as wicked murders, or has perpetrated other deeds like them, akin to them and to the deeds of kindred souls, then each and all flee from her, and avoid her, and no one will become her comrade on the journey or her guide; alone she wanders, utterly forlorn, till certain times be accomplished; and when they are fulfilled, she is borne perforce to the abode befitting her. But the soul that has passed through life in purity and temperance has gods for her comrades and guides, and abides in the special place befitting her. The earth has many wonderful regions in it, and neither in its nature nor its size is it as they opine who are in the habit of discussing it; of this a certain person has convinced me.'

[SIMMIAS.] 'What have you in mind now, Socrates?' said Simmias. 'I too have heard a great deal said about the earth, but not what you believe; so I should be very glad to hear it.'

[SOCRATES.] 'Now, Simmias, I do not think that I need the system of Glaucus in order to explain what I believe. But what the truth is seems to me a harder thing to explain than it is by Glaucus' system. And meanwhile very likely I am not competent to do it, or, supposing I really had the knowledge, Simmias, I think that I have not long enough to live to finish the explanation. But there is nothing to prevent my telling what I believe the form of the earth to be, or what the regions of it are.'

[SIMMIAS.] 'But that,' said Simmias, 'is quite enough.'

[SOCRATES.] 'Well, first of all,' said he, 'I am convinced that if the earth is at the centre of the heaven, and is spherical, then it has no need of air or any similar force to prevent its falling. Rather, the equiformity of the heaven itself in all directions, and the equilibrium of the earth itself, are enough to hold it in position; for a thing that is in equilibrium, and placed in the middle of a uniform container, cannot incline in one direction more than in another, but must remain in one position and in balance. That,' said he, 'is the first point of which I am convinced.'

[SIMMIAS.] 'And rightly, too,' said Simmias.

[SOCRATES.] 'Furthermore,' said he, 'I hold that this body is of vast extent, and that we who dwell between the river Phasis and the pillars of Heracles [from the Black Sea to Gibraltar] inhabit but a little part of it, living about our [Mediterranean] Sea like ants or frogs about a pond. And elsewhere there are many other men, living in many comparable places; for throughout the surface of the earth there are numerous basins of every shape and size, into which the water, vapor, and air collect together. The earth itself [its proper, higher, surface] is pure, and lies in the pure heaven, in which are the stars [including sun and moon], that which the generality of those who are wont to discuss such matters call the ether [the sky of blue fire]. The dregs of this ether are the things in question which constantly flow together into the basins of the earth. Accordingly, we dwell in the said basins without knowing it, and think that we are dwelling on the surface of the earth; it is just as if a man were living at the bottom of the sea, in the middle, and thought that he was living on the surface of it, and seeing the sun and all the stars through the water, took the sea to be the heaven. From lethargy and weakness he never would come to the top of the sea, nor emerge and lift his head above it to look into our region here and note how much more pure and beautiful it is than the habitation of his kind; nor would he have heard about it from anybody else. That is just our situation. We are living in a basin of the earth, but think that we are living on the surface, and we call the air the sky, supposing this to be the heaven where the stars move in their courses. It is the same with us. From our weakness and our lethargy we cannot pass through to the surface of the air; for if anybody reached the top of it, or grew wings and flew up thither, and put out his head, then just as here below the fishes put their heads out of the sea, and behold things here below, so would he behold the things up yonder. And if our nature were sufficient to endure the sight, he would know that he was looking at the real heaven, the true light, and the veritable earth; for our earth here, the stones, and every region here below—it all is decayed and corroded, as what the sea holds is corroded by the brine; and nothing worth mention is brought forth in the sea, nothing perfect, so to speak, is there; but wherever there is land, only rocky caverns, sand, and unimaginable tracts of mud and slime; nought of any value whatsoever in comparison with the things of beauty here. But those on high would shine out eminent, far more beautiful than ours below. If this is a good point for a story, Simmias, I can tell one that is worth the hearing, on the kind of things to be found upon [that surface of] the earth which is just beneath the heaven.'

110

[SIMMIAS.]   'Indeed, Socrates,' said Simmias, 'we should very much like to hear this story.'

[SOCRATES.]   'Well, my friend,' said he, 'this is the way it goes. First of all, the earth itself, when viewed from above, looks like one of those leathern balls made of twelve pieces, variegated, diversified with colors of which the colors here below are samples, these being what the painters use. But there the whole earth has such colors, only they are far, far brighter and purer than these. There, one part is purple and of a marvelous beauty, another golden, another—all the white part—whiter than chalk or snow; and so with all the other colors of which it is made up, more colors, and more beautiful, than any we ever saw. As for the aforesaid basins of it, being filled with water and air, from above they have a color of their own, gleaming in the pattern of the rest, and so the earth is seen as one continuous, many-colored surface. And in that earth so constituted, whatever grows is in proportion fairer than what grows with us, trees and flowers and fruits; and similarly the mountains and the stones, in the same proportion, are more beautiful for their smoothness, their transparency, their color. The pebbles here below, the jewels we so highly prize, carnelian, jasper, emerald, and all the like, are merely bits of them; yonder every stone is like a jewel, only they are fairer yet than ours. The reason for it is that they are pure, and not corroded or decayed, as are the stones with us, through rot and brine because of the mixture that has run together here; this it is that alike to stones and earth, and all the animals and plants, has brought deformity and disease. But the real earth is adorned with all these things, with gold as well, and silver, and, in fine, with everything else of the sort. By nature they are exposed to sight, so plentiful, so large, so scattered everywhere throughout the earth, that to see it is a spectacle for the contemplation of the blest. There are many living creatures on it besides men; of the men, some dwell in the interior, others on the shore of the air, as we do by the sea, others on islands surrounded by the·air, adjacent to the mainland. In a word, there they use the air as we use water and the sea, and the ether as we use the air. The climate in all seasons is so mild that they are free from sickness, and live much longer than do people here; and in sight and hearing and intelligence, and all similar functions, they excel us to the same extent that the air in purity surpasses water, and the ether surpasses the air. Moreover they have groves and temples of the gods in which gods actually dwell; they hear the sacred voices and the prophecies, and have direct perception of the gods, and thus are in communion with them face to face. And the sun and the moon and the stars are seen by them as they really are. And in all else their happiness accords with all of that.

'Such is the general nature of the earth and of that which appertains to it. The regions in it, answering to its hollows, and disposed round its circumference, are numerous in relation to the whole; some are deeper and broader than the one we live in; others, while deeper, have a narrower outline than our own region; still others have less depth than this, and greater breadth. Now all these regions communicate with one another variously by subterranean tunnels narrower and wider, and they have passages whereby much water flows from one into another as into bowls, and there run perennial rivers of immeasurable size below the earth, of water both hot and cold. Much fire there is, and huge rivers of fire; and many rivers of liquid mud, clearer some, others more turbid, like the streams of mud in Sicily that come before the lava, and then the lava-stream itself. These rivers severally fill each several space to which the individual river in its circuit, according to its motion, comes. But that which causes all this motion up and down is a kind of see-saw that is in the earth, and this oscillation is produced by natural conditions of the following sort.

'One of the chasms in the earth is larger than all the rest, and pierces straight through it from one side to the other. This it is that Homer describes, when [*Iliad* 8.14] he says it is 112

> Far off, where lies the nethermost abyss below the earth;

which elsewhere he and many another of the poets have called Tartarus. All the rivers run together to this chasm, and run out of it again; and they severally gain their individual character from the sort of earth through which they run. But the reason why these streams all flow from that one chasm, and flow into it, is that the liquid has no bottom or base to rest on; and so it oscillates and surges up and down. And the air and the wind adjacent do the same, for they accompany the liquid in its sweep to the far side of the earth, as well as in its sweep to ours; and just as in the act

of breathing, the stream of air is constantly exhaled and then in-
haled, so there: the air accompanying the liquid in its oscillation
produces terrible and irresistible blasts, alike as it is going in and
coming out. So when the water goes off into the region commonly
referred to as "below," the streams flow through the earth to those
parts aforesaid, and fill them up; it is like the work of men who
irrigate. When, on the other hand, the water comes away from there,
and rushes hither, it fills these parts again. Once they are filled, the
streams run through the tunnels and through the earth, and, severally arriving at the individual places into which their way is made,
form seas, lakes, rivers, and springs; from there the streams sink
into the earth again, and, after running, some of them, round
greater and more numerous spaces, some round fewer and shorter,
once more fall into Tartarus, some at a level much lower than the
one from which they were pumped out, others but a little lower;
but the point of inflow in all cases is lower than the exit. And some
of them break out on the opposite side [of the centre of the earth]
from the point where they flow in, and some on the same side;
while there are some that once or more than once describe a spiral
course around the earth, enfolding it like snakes, and then descend
to the deepest level possible to fall in again. It is possible for the
liquid to descend, on either side [of the centre], as far down as the
centre, but not beyond it; for the part on either side of it is up-hill
for both sets of streams.

'Accordingly, the streams are many, mighty, and diverse; but
in this multitude there are four to be distinguished, of which the
greatest, which describes the circle furthest from the centre, is the
one they call Oceanus. Diametrically opposite to it, and flowing
in the opposite direction, is the Acheron; this runs through desert
regions, and then beneath the surface, till it comes to the Acherusian
lake. That is where the souls of the majority come after they are
dead; and when they have remained there for such times as are
appointed, longer for some, for others shorter, they are again sent
forth to be reborn as animals. A third river issues [out of Tartarus]
at a point between these two, and near its exit falls into a vast and
fiery region full of flames, and forms a lake, larger than our sea

here, of boiling water and mud; thence, turbid and muddy, it coils itself round inside the earth in a spiral, and arrives in another region at the end of the Acherusian lake, but not commingling with its waters; and after many windings in a spiral under the earth, falls into Tartarus at a lower point. This is the river to which they give the name of Pyriphlegethon; and it is the lava-streams of this that send detached portions where the like occur on earth. On the opposite side of the centre from Pyriphlegethon, the fourth stream issues first into a region which, according to report, is terrible and savage, all of a color like blue steel; this is the region they call Stygian, and the river forms the Stygian lake which it falls into. When it has entered the lake, and there acquired strange powers in the water, it sinks down in the earth, and, taking a spiral course in a direction opposite to Pyriphlegethon, approaches the Acherusian lake from the opposite side [to the aforesaid river]; nor does its water mingle with another, but this river, too, moving in a curve falls into Tartarus on the opposite side [of the centre] to Pyriphlegethon. The name of this river, as the poets have it, is Cocytus.

'Such is the nature of those regions; and when the departed reach the place to which the genius of each one severally guides them, first of all they have sentence passed on them, those who have lived beautiful and holy lives along with those who have not. And they who, it would seem, have lived a middling life go to the river Acheron, and there embarking on the boats provided for them, proceed to the lake, and, dwelling there, are purified, and by the penalty they pay for any wrongs they may have done, get absolution, while obtaining for good deeds their due reward, each one according to his desert. But they who are seen to be incurable from the magnitude of their offences, who repeatedly have done great sacrilege, or committed many foul and lawless murders, or done any similar misdeeds; for them it is their fitting lot to be hurled down into Tartarus, whence they nevermore come forth. They, however, who are seen to have committed sins which, while great, are not incurable; they, for instance, who in anger have done violence to a father or a mother, but thereafter have spent their life 114 repenting, or who in other similar circumstances have committed murder; these must, perforce, fall into Tartarus. But thereafter, when a year has passed, the upsurge casts them forth, the homicides by Cocytus, those violent to a father or a mother by Pyriphlegethon. And when they have been carried to the level of the Acherusian lake, there they cry aloud, and call on those whom they have slain, or those whom they have outraged, and, having summoned them, implore and beg their victims to let them come out into the lake, and to receive them. And if they prevail, they come out, and their pains are at an end. If not, they are carried back to Tartarus, and thence once more into the rivers, and thus they go on suffering till they prevail with those whom they have wronged; for such is the penalty that is laid upon them by the Judges. But those who have been eminent for the holy lives they lived, they it is who are released from these interior regions of the earth, and set free as from a prison; and, rising, they attain to the pure habitation, and dwell upon the [real surface of the] earth. And those among them who have adequately purified themselves with philosophy live thenceforth absolutely without bodies, and proceed to dwellings lovelier yet than these [in the heavens], dwellings such as are not easily described, nor, at present, is there time enough to do it.

'But, Simmias, on all these grounds which we have now traversed, it behoves us to do everything in order to participate in virtue and in wisdom in our life; for noble is the guerdon, and the hope is great! Meanwhile it will not do for a man of sense to insist that all these things are exactly as I have described them. But that this or something of the sort is true of our souls and the places where they dwell, since, as it most certainly appears, the spirit is immortal —that, to my mind, it is right and proper for a man to risk believing. The chance is beautiful, and it is fitting for him to charm his thought with suchlike minstrelsy; that is why this long while now I have lengthened out the tale. There, however, lies the reason why that man should have no fear about his soul, who in his life has renounced the pleasures and embellishments of the body as alien to him, and, in his judgment, more apt to do him harm than good; but who has eagerly pursued the joys of learning, and, adorning his soul, not with alien, but with her own proper ornaments,

namely, temperance and justice and courage and freedom and truth, 115
thus awaits the journey into Hades, ready to set forth whenever
his allotted call shall come. You, Simmias and Cebes,' he continued,
'you and all the rest, hereafter will set forth, each at a certain time.
Me, as a tragic character would say, my destiny now calls; and the
hour is nigh for me to go and take a bath—for I think I had better
bathe before I drink the poison, and save the women the trouble of
washing a dead body.'

[CRITO.] When he had finished speaking, Crito said: 'So be it,
Socrates. But have you any directions that you wish to give to the
rest here, or to me, about your children, or on any other matter—
anything at all that we can do for love of you?'

[SOCRATES.] 'Nothing more than what I have kept telling you,
Crito,' said he; 'nothing new. Simply care for your own real welfare, and you will do for me and mine, and for yourselves, all that
love could ask; no need of promising it now. If you do not care for
your own real selves, and will not live according to the principles,
step for step, which we have traced to-day and heretofore, it will
be of no avail, however many solemn promises you may make at
present.'

[CRITO.] 'We shall try with all our might,' said he, 'to do this thing.
But how are we to bury you?'

[SOCRATES.] 'Any way you like,' said he, 'if you can catch me, and I
do n't get away from you.' And, with a quiet laugh, he looked at us
and said: 'Gentlemen, I cannot convince Crito that I am the Socrates
who has been talking with you, and putting each and all his arguments in proper sequence. No, he thinks I am that object which
shortly he will see as a dead body, and asks how he shall inter that
"me." What has happened to the ample argument I have all this
while been making, to prove that, after I have drunk the
poison, I shall no longer be with you, but, departing, shall go away
to the joys of the blest? It would seem that for him I said it all
simply to comfort you, simply to comfort myself as well. Do you
therefore be sureties to Crito for me,' said he, 'as he was my surety
to the judges; but with the opposite intent, for he went surety that
I would stay here, while you are to be sureties that when I die, I

certainly shall not stay here, but shall depart and go my way. You will thus help Crito more easily to bear it, and when he sees my body burnt or buried, he will not grieve for me as if he thought that I was suffering something dreadful, nor at the obsequies say that it is Socrates that he is laying out, or carrying to the grave, or burying; for, admirable Crito! rest assured that wrongful usage does not merely injure speech itself, but introduces harm into our souls as well. No, you must have no fear, and say it is the funeral of my body, and must have the funeral as you prefer it, and as you think will best conform to custom.'

[PHAEDO.]   So saying, he rose and went into another room to bathe; and Crito followed him, telling us to wait. So we waited, talking among ourselves about the argument, and weighing it again, then coming back to dwell upon the great calamity that had befallen us. To us, it was indeed as if we were about to lose a father, and were thenceforth going to be orphans all our life. When he had bathed, and they had brought his children to him—he had two little boys, and a third who was well-grown—and the women of his family had come, he talked with them in Crito's presence, and gave them such instructions as he wished. Then he caused the women and the children to be sent away, while he returned to us.

By now it was near sunset; for he had spent a long time within. Coming to us, with his body washed, he took his seat, and nothing much was said thereafter. Then the servant of the Eleven came, and, stepping up to him, said: 'Socrates, I know that I need not expect from you what I expect to get from others; for they rage and curse at me, when I come to bid them drink the poison, under compulsion from the magistrates. But I have found you all along the noblest and gentlest and best man of all who ever reached this place; and now I am sure that you will not be angry with me, but with those who are responsible, as you know. Now then, you know what I have come to tell you. So fare you well, and try to bear what must be as lightly as you can.' Then bursting into tears, he turned away, and went out.

And Socrates looked up, and answered him: 'You too,' said he, 'farewell! And we will follow your advice.' Then, turning to us, he said: 'How considerate the man is! And the whole time I have been here he has come to see me, and occasionally talked with me, and has been as good as he could be; and now, how generously he weeps for me! Come, Crito, let us do his bidding; let the poison be brought, if they have it ready. If not, let the man prepare it.'

[CRITO.] 'But, Socrates,' said Crito, 'I think the sun is still upon the mountains, and is not yet down. Besides, I know that others have not taken the draft till late, long after word was brought to them. They have eaten and drunk well, after having had the company of such persons as they specially desired. Do not hurry; there is still some time.'

[SOCRATES.] 'For the men you speak of, Crito,' he replied, 'it is natural that they should do so, for they think that they will gain by doing it. As for me, I naturally shall not do it, for I think I can gain nothing if I take the draft a little later; I could only make 117 myself ridiculous in my own eyes by clinging to this life and saving some when there was nothing left. Come now,' he said; 'do as I wish, and do n't refuse me.'

[PHAEDO.] And Crito thereupon made a sign to his servant who was standing near. The servant then went out, and after some delay came back with the man that was to give the poison, who was carrying it prepared in a cup. When Socrates saw the man, he said: 'Well done, my friend. You understand these things; so tell me what to do.' 'Simply this,' he said. 'When you have drunk it, walk around until your legs grow heavy; then lie down. In that way it will do its work.' With that he handed Socrates the cup. He took it, and, Echecrates, quite cheerfully, without a tremor or any change of color, or alteration in his face, but looking at the man askance in his ironic fashion, asked: 'What say you? Is it lawful that we make libation from this beverage to a god? Or must we not?' 'Socrates,' he said, 'we prepare no more than what we think will be the right amount.' 'I understand,' he answered. 'But, at all events, no doubt I may, I must, pray to the gods that my change of abode from hence to the world beyond shall be attended by success. That is my prayer; so be it!' So saying, he put the cup to his lips, and with great ease, without the least aversion, he drained the contents down.

Till then, most of us had succeeded fairly well in holding back our tears; but when we saw him drinking, when we saw that it was done, we could refrain no longer. As for me, in spite of all, my tears came gushing, so I covered my head and wept—for myself; it was not for him, but for thinking of my own calamity, I was losing such a friend. Crito, even before me, found himself unable to keep back his tears, and got up to go away; and Apollodorus, who had never once ceased weeping all the while, now broke out into loud and bitter cries, until everybody who was there broke down, save only Socrates himself. 'What in the world are you doing, my friends?' he exclaimed. 'I sent the women away mainly in order to avoid their misbehaving in this way; for I have been told that a man should die in peace. Be quiet, and hold fast.' When we heard that, we were ashamed, and stopped our crying.

But he walked about, until he said that his legs were getting heavy; then he lay down upon his back, as he had been directed, and the man at intervals examined him, feeling of his feet and legs. Then, pressing hard against his foot, he asked him if he felt it. Socrates said, 'No'; and after that he did it to his shins, and moving upwards, showed us that he was growing cold and stiff, and, touching Socrates, he said that when it reached the heart, he would be gone. Already he was growing cold below the navel, when he uncovered his face—for he had covered it—and spoke— they were his last words: 'Crito,' he said, 'we owe a cock to Aesculapius; [10] you must not forget to pay it.' 'It shall be done,' said Crito. 'Can you think of anything else?' To this question he made no reply; but in a little while there was a convulsive movement, after which the man uncovered him. His eyes were fixed. When Crito saw, he closed the mouth and eyes.

Such was the end, Echecrates, of him who was our comrade; a man of whom we may well say that among all the men we ever knew he was the best, and also the most wise and just.

[10] The god of medicine; Socrates is grateful to him for the freedom his soul is gaining from the body.

A Brief List of Books for the Study of Plato

AST, FRIEDRICH. *Lexicon Platonicum.* Leipsic, 1835-6-8.

BERNAYS, JACOB. *Die Dialoge des Aristoteles in ihrem Verhältniss zu seinen übrigen Werken.* Berlin, 1863.

BURNET, JOHN. *Platonism.* Berkeley, 1928.

———— *Plato's Phaedo.* Edited, with Introduction and Notes. Oxford, 1911 (impression of 1931).

CAMERON, ALISTER. *The Pythagorean Background of the Theory of Recollection.* Menasha, Wisconsin (George Banta), 1938.

COOPER, LANE. *Louis Agassiz as a Teacher.* Ithaca, 1917.

———— *Two Views of Education.* New Haven, 1922.

———— *An Aristotelian Theory of Comedy.* New York, 1922.

———— *Evolution and Repentance.* Ithaca, 1935.

———— *Plato; Phaedrus, Ion, Gorgias, and Symposium, with Passages from the Republic and Laws;* Translated into English, with an Introduction and Prefatory Notes. New York, 1938.

———— *Our Plato.* In *The Classical Bulletin* (St. Louis) 16 (1940). 25-7, 32.

DEMETRIUS. *On Style. The Greek Text of Demetrius De Elocutione.* Ed. and trans. by W. Rhys Roberts. Cambridge, 1902.

DIONYSIUS OF HALICARNASSUS. *On Literary Composition.* Ed. and trans. by W. Rhys Roberts. London, 1910.

FIELD, GUY CROMWELL. *Plato and his Contemporaries; a Study in Fourth-Century Life and Thought.* London, 1930.

FRYE, PROSSER HALL. *Plato. The University Studies of the University of Nebraska.* Volume 38. Lincoln, 1938.

GILSON, ÉTIENNE. *The Spirit of Mediæval Philosophy.* New York, 1936.

HARWARD, JOHN. *The Platonic Epistles, translated, with Introduction and· Notes.* Cambridge, 1932.

HIRZEL, RUDOLF. *Der Dialog; ein Literarhistorischer Versuch.* 2 vols. Leipsic, 1895.

HYDE, WILLIAM DE WITT. *The Five Great Philosophies of Life*. New York, 1911.

'LONGINUS.' *On the Sublime*. Ed. and trans. by W. Rhys Roberts. Second ed. Cambridge, 1907.

LUTOSLAWSKI, WINCENTY. *The Origin and Growth of Plato's Logic; with an Account of Plato's Style, and of the Chronology of his Writings*. New York, 1897.

OLDFATHER, WILLIAM A. *Socrates in Court*. In *Classical Weekly* 31 (1938). 203–11.

REICH, HERMANN. *Der Mimus; ein Litterar-entwickelungsgeschichtlicher Versuch*. Berlin, 1903.

RITTER, CONSTANTIN. *The Essence of Plato's Philosophy*. Trans. by Adam Alles. London, 1933.

SHEBBEARE, C. J. *The Problem of the Future Life*. Oxford, 1939.

SHOREY, PAUL. *What Plato Said*. Chicago, 1933.

—— *Platonism, Ancient and Modern*. Berkeley, 1938.

STEWART, J. A. *The Myths of Plato*. London, 1905.

TAYLOR, A. E. *Plato, the Man and his Work*. New York, 1927.

XENOPHON. *The Memorabilia, or Recollections of Socrates; the Apology of Socrates; the Economist; Symposium, or the Banquet. The Works of Xenophon*, translated by H. G. Dakyns, Vol. 3, Part 1. London, 1897.

Index

The names of Socrates and Plato are here omitted save for three cases where Plato is mentioned by speakers in dialogue. A few items in the Preface are included in the Index because of their relation to the substance of the book. Names in the list of dates on pp. xiii-xiv, and in the list of books on pp. 193-4, are omitted, as are some names and titles in footnotes, and references to the word 'soul.'